HEROIC ANIMALS

SERGEANT RECKLESS

BRAVES THE BATTLEFIELD

HEROIC KOREAN WAR HORSE

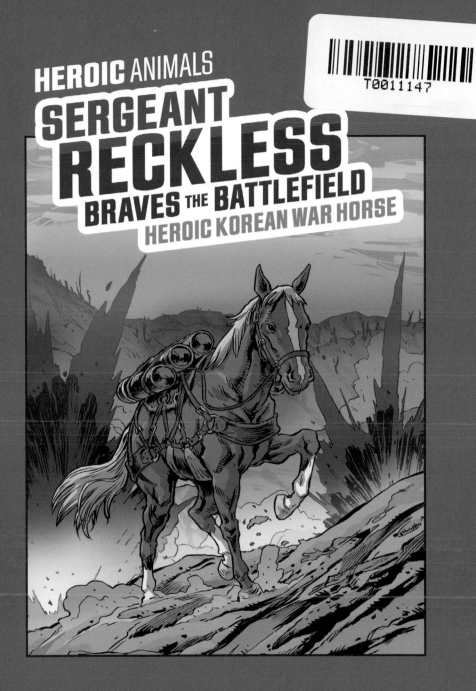

BY **BRUCE BERGLUND**   ILLUSTRATED BY **MARK SIMMONS**

CAPSTONE PRESS
a capstone imprint

Published by Capstone Press, an imprint of Capstone.
1710 Roe Crest Drive, North Mankato, Minnesota 56003
capstonepub.com

Library of Congress Cataloging-in-Publication Data
Names: Berglund, Bruce R., author. | Simmons, Mark, illustrator.
Title: Sergeant Reckless braves the battlefield : heroic Korean war horse / by Bruce Berglund ; illustrated by Mark Simmons.
Other titles: Heroic Korean war horse
Description: North Mankato, Minnesota : Capstone Press, an imprint of Capstone, [2023] | Series: Heroic animals | Includes bibliographical references. | Audience: Ages 8-11 | Audience: Grades 4-6
Summary: "In 1952, the United States was heavily involved in the Korean War. When members of the U.S. Marine Corps bought a horse to join in the war effort, little did they know that a hero would soon emerge. Trained to be a military pack horse, Sergeant Reckless quickly became a part of the unit and served to support the troops in several combat missions during the war. Discover the heroic story of Sergeant Reckless as she bravely made many solo trips during battles to deliver supplies to troops on the front lines"-- Provided by publisher.
Identifiers: LCCN 2022024618 (print) | LCCN 2022024619 (ebook) | ISBN 9781666394009 (hardcover) | ISBN 9781666394153 (paperback) | ISBN 9781666393996 (ebook PDF) | ISBN 9781666394177 (kindle edition)
Subjects: LCSH: Sergeant Reckless (Horse), approximately 1948-1968--Juvenile literature. | Korean War, 1950-1953--Participation, American--Juvenile literature. | War horses--United States--Juvenile literature. | War horses--Korea (South)--Juvenile literature. | United States. Marine Corps--Juvenile literature.
Classification: LCC DS919 .B474 2023 (print) | LCC DS919 (ebook) | DDC 951.904/2373--dc23/eng/20220610
LC record available at https://lccn.loc.gov/2022024618
LC ebook record available at https://lccn.loc.gov/2022024619

Editorial Credits
Editor: Aaron Sautter; Designer: Elyse White; Media Researcher: Rebekah Hubstenberger; Production Specialist: Whitney Schaefer

Photo Credit
Getty Images: Bettmann, 29

All internet sites appearing in back matter were available and accurate when this book was sent to press.

Direct quotes appear in ***bold, italicized*** text on the following pages:

Page 11: Geer, Andrew Clare. *Reckless: Pride of the Marines*. New York: Dutton, 1955.
Pages 12, 13, 25, 26: Hutton, Robin L. *Sgt. Reckless: America's War Horse*. Washington, D.C.: Regnery Publishing, 2014.

Printed and bound in the USA. PO# 5195

TABLE OF CONTENTS

Chapter 1: Horsepower in Modern War

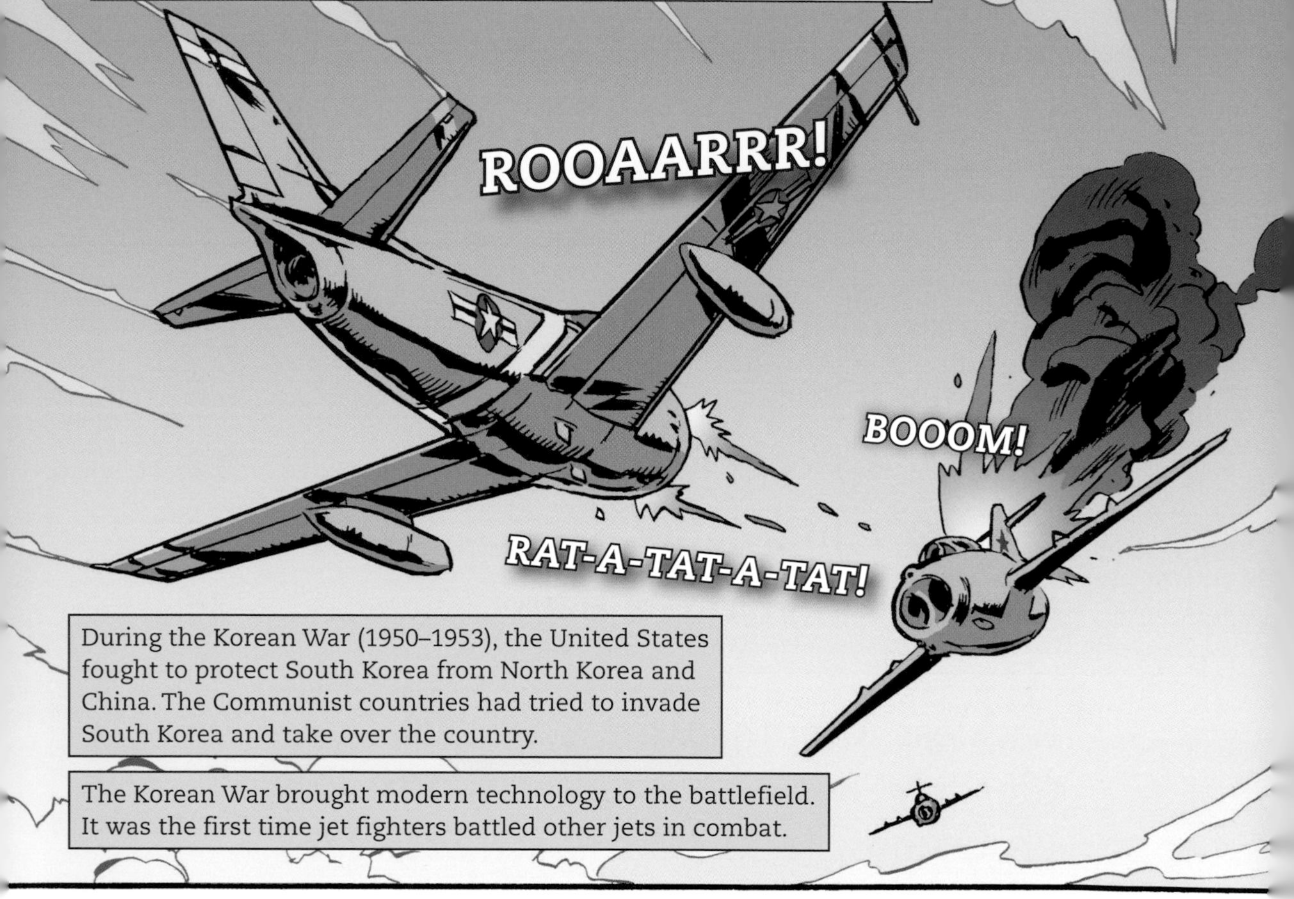
ROOAARRR!
BOOOM!
RAT-A-TAT-A-TAT!
During the Korean War (1950–1953), the United States fought to protect South Korea from North Korea and China. The Communist countries had tried to invade South Korea and take over the country.
The Korean War brought modern technology to the battlefield. It was the first time jet fighters battled other jets in combat.

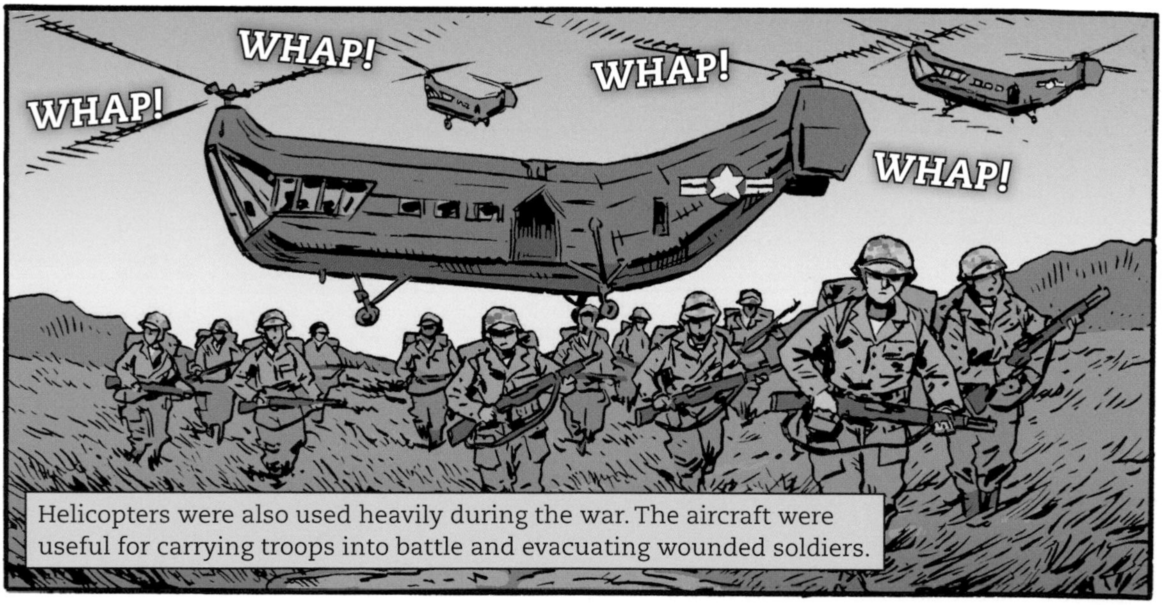
WHAP!
WHAP!
WHAP!
WHAP!
Helicopters were also used heavily during the war. The aircraft were useful for carrying troops into battle and evacuating wounded soldiers.

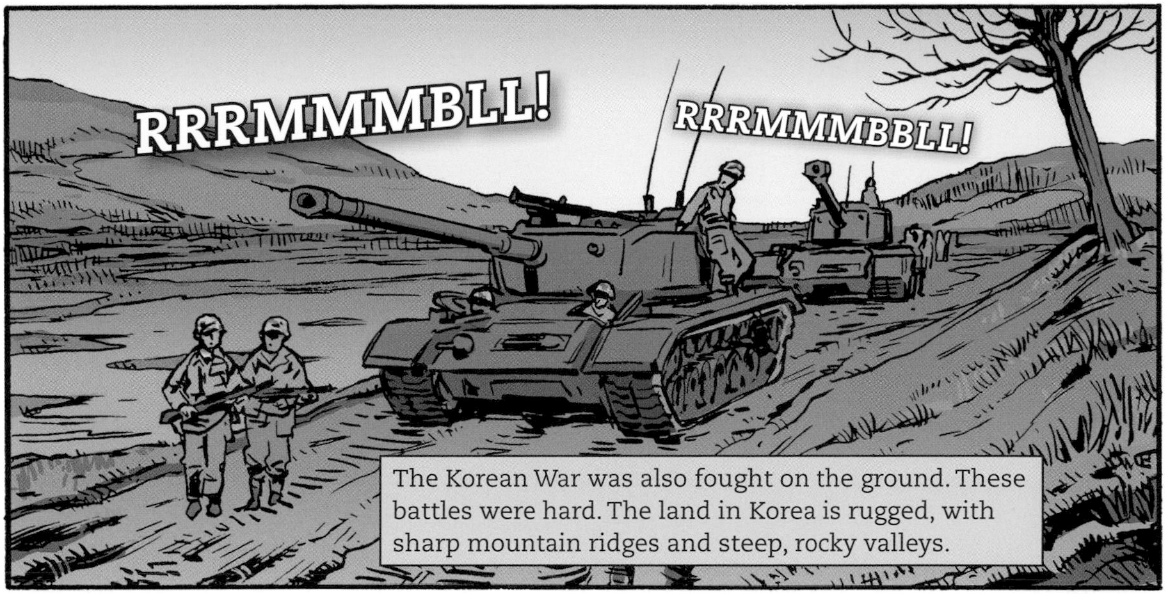
RRRMMMMBLL!
RRRMMMMBBLL!
The Korean War was also fought on the ground. These battles were hard. The land in Korea is rugged, with sharp mountain ridges and steep, rocky valleys.

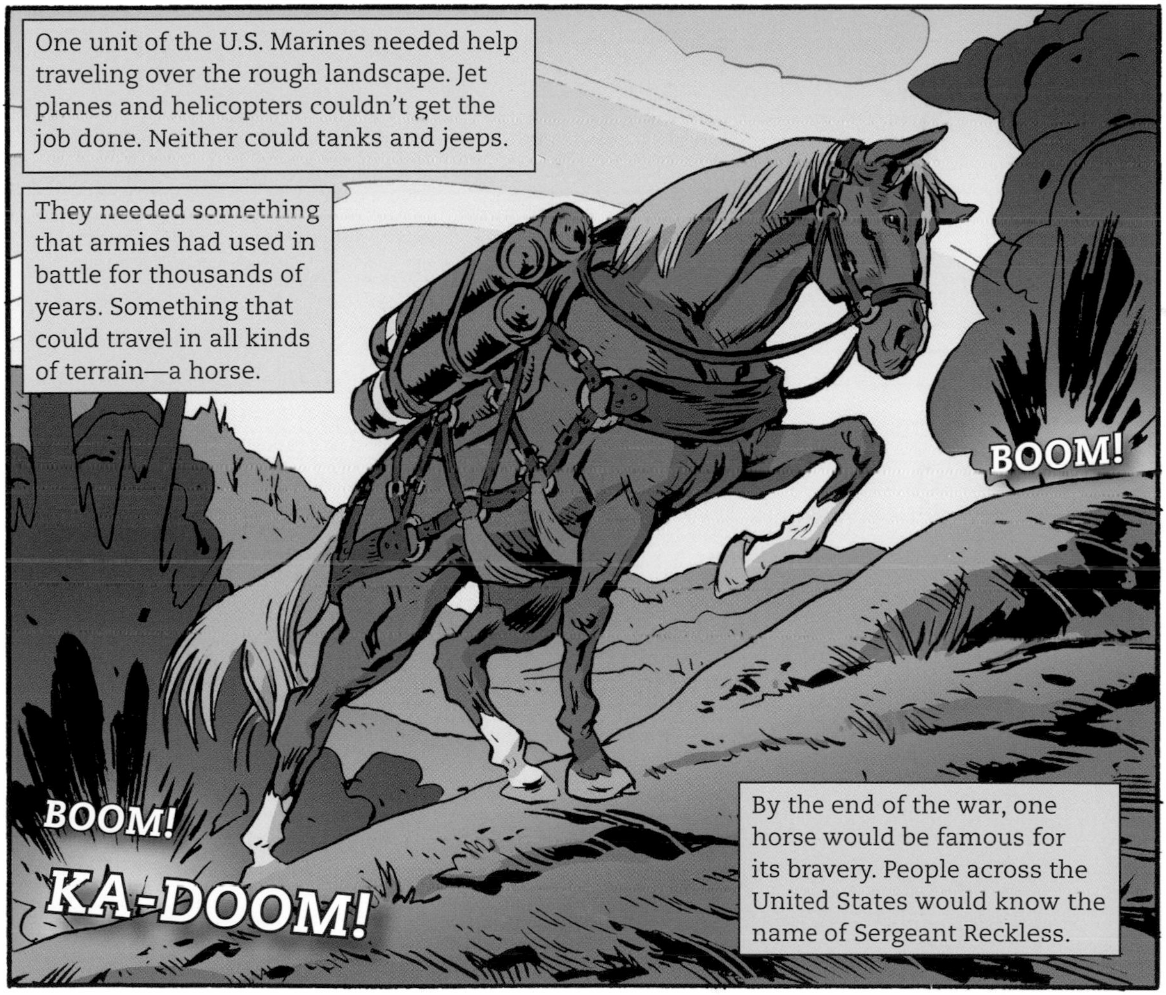
One unit of the U.S. Marines needed help traveling over the rough landscape. Jet planes and helicopters couldn't get the job done. Neither could tanks and jeeps.
They needed something that armies had used in battle for thousands of years. Something that could travel in all kinds of terrain—a horse.
BOOM!
BOOM!
KA-DOOM!
By the end of the war, one horse would be famous for its bravery. People across the United States would know the name of Sergeant Reckless.

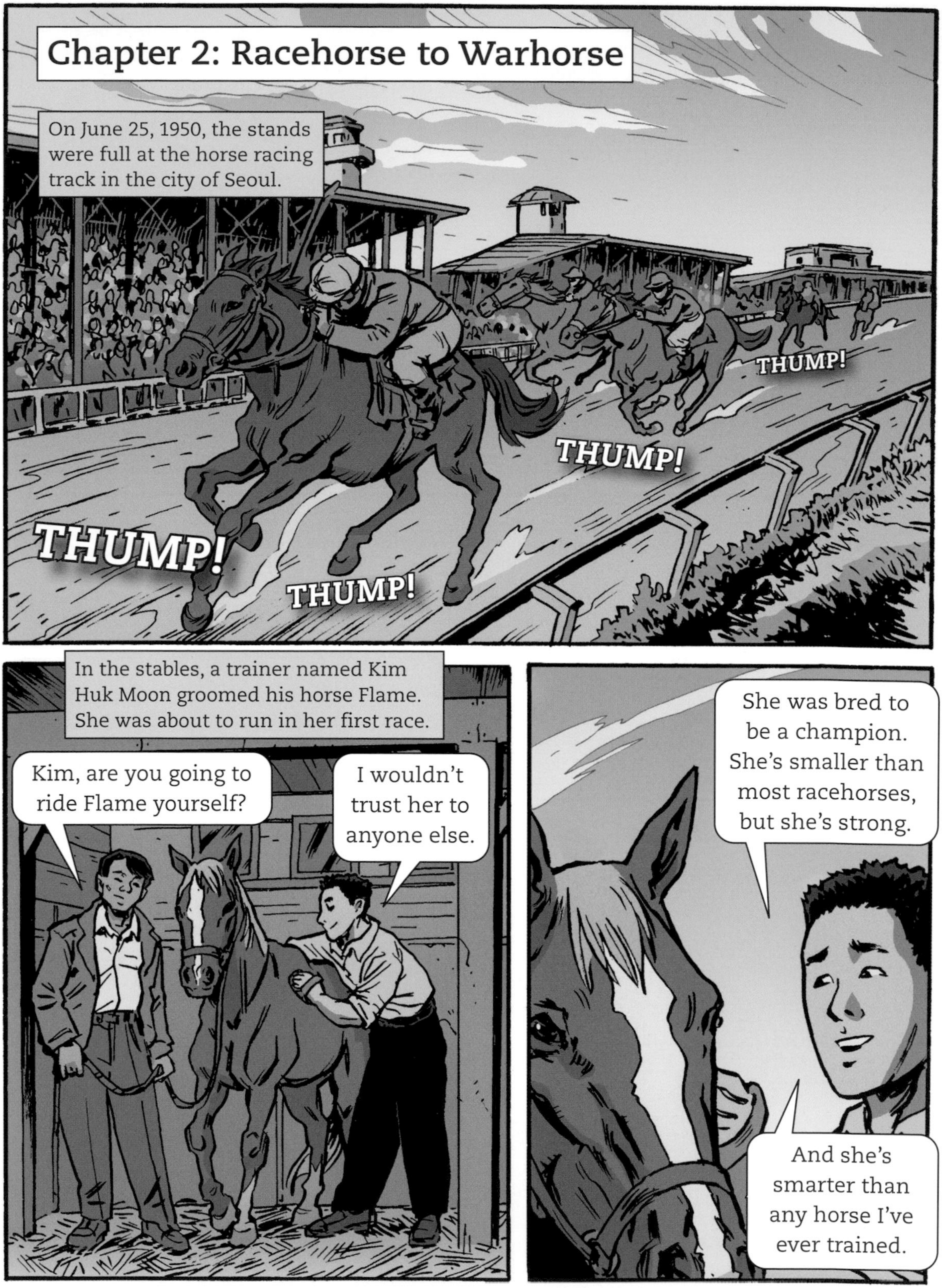
Chapter 2: Racehorse to Warhorse
On June 25, 1950, the stands were full at the horse racing track in the city of Seoul.
THUMP!
THUMP!
THUMP!
THUMP!
In the stables, a trainer named Kim Huk Moon groomed his horse Flame. She was about to run in her first race.
Kim, are you going to ride Flame yourself?
I wouldn't trust her to anyone else.
She was bred to be a champion. She's smaller than most racehorses, but she's strong.
And she's smarter than any horse I've ever trained.

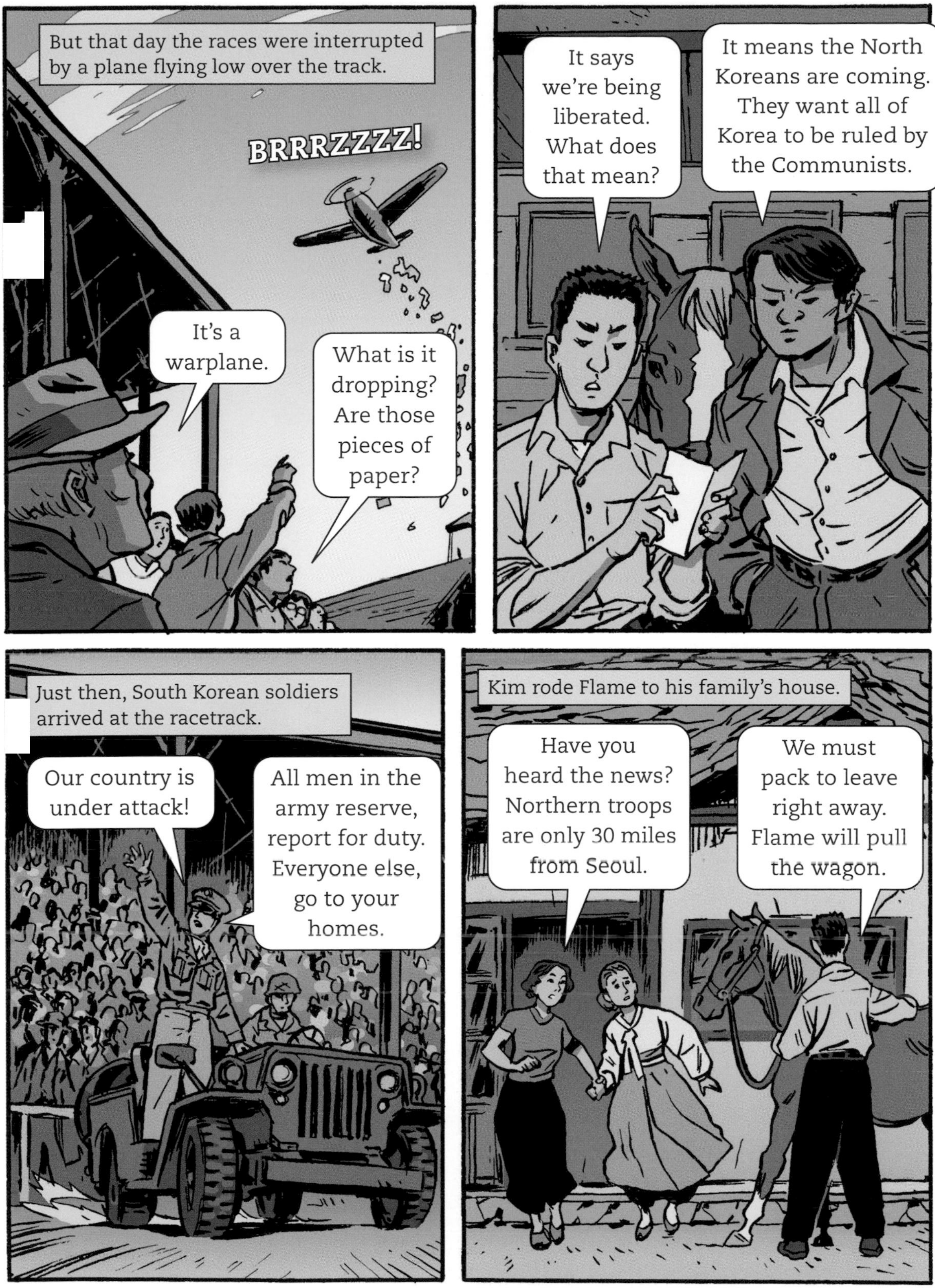
But that day the races were interrupted by a plane flying low over the track.
BRRRZZZZ!
It's a warplane.
What is it dropping? Are those pieces of paper?
It says we're being liberated. What does that mean?
It means the North Koreans are coming. They want all of Korea to be ruled by the Communists.
Just then, South Korean soldiers arrived at the racetrack.
Our country is under attack!
All men in the army reserve, report for duty. Everyone else, go to your homes.
Kim rode Flame to his family's house.
Have you heard the news? Northern troops are only 30 miles from Seoul.
We must pack to leave right away. Flame will pull the wagon.

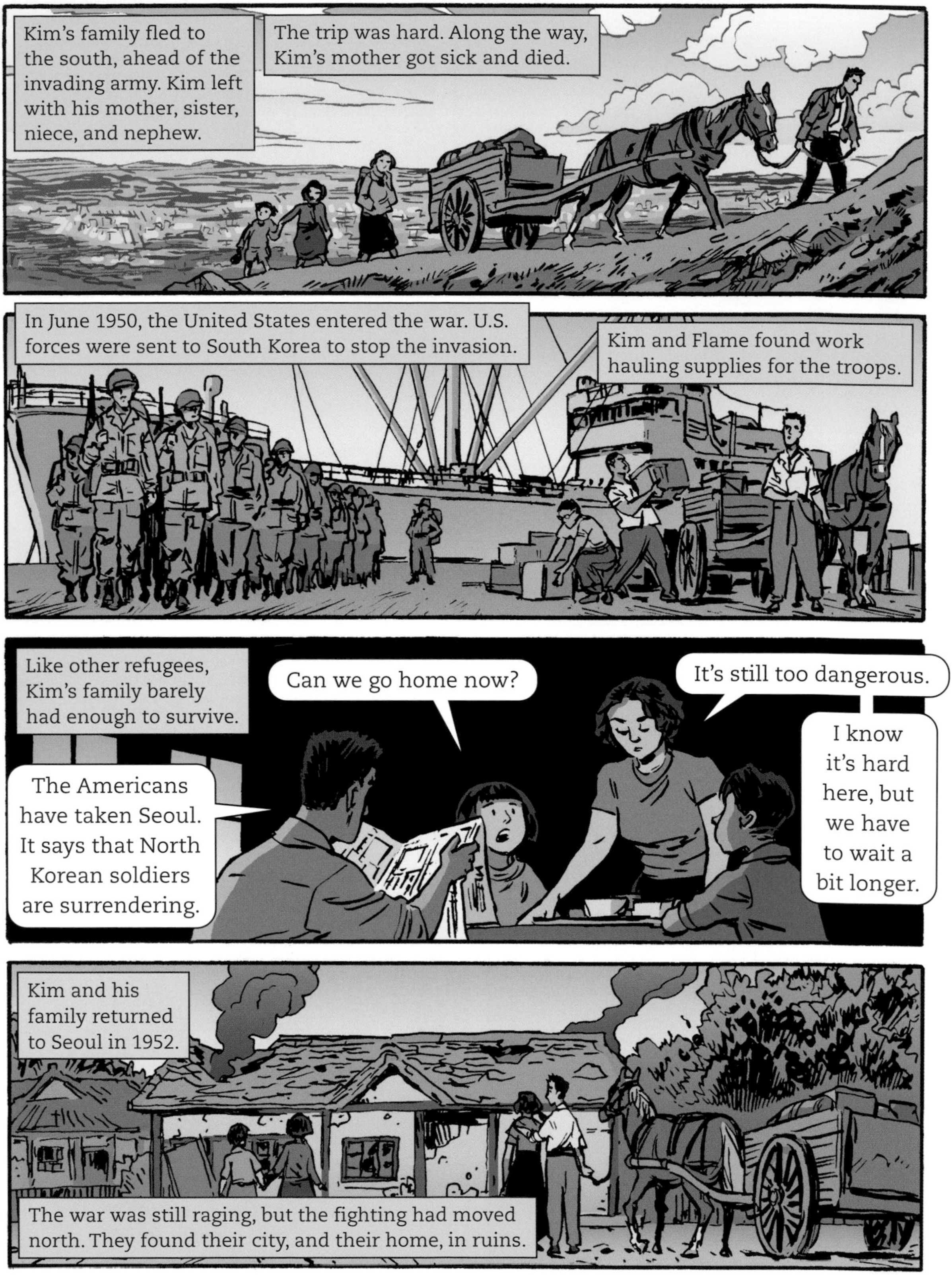
Kim's family fled to the south, ahead of the invading army. Kim left with his mother, sister, niece, and nephew.
The trip was hard. Along the way, Kim's mother got sick and died.
In June 1950, the United States entered the war. U.S. forces were sent to South Korea to stop the invasion.
Kim and Flame found work hauling supplies for the troops.
Like other refugees, Kim's family barely had enough to survive.
Can we go home now?
It's still too dangerous.
I know it's hard here, but we have to wait a bit longer.
The Americans have taken Seoul. It says that North Korean soldiers are surrendering.
Kim and his family returned to Seoul in 1952.
The war was still raging, but the fighting had moved north. They found their city, and their home, in ruins.

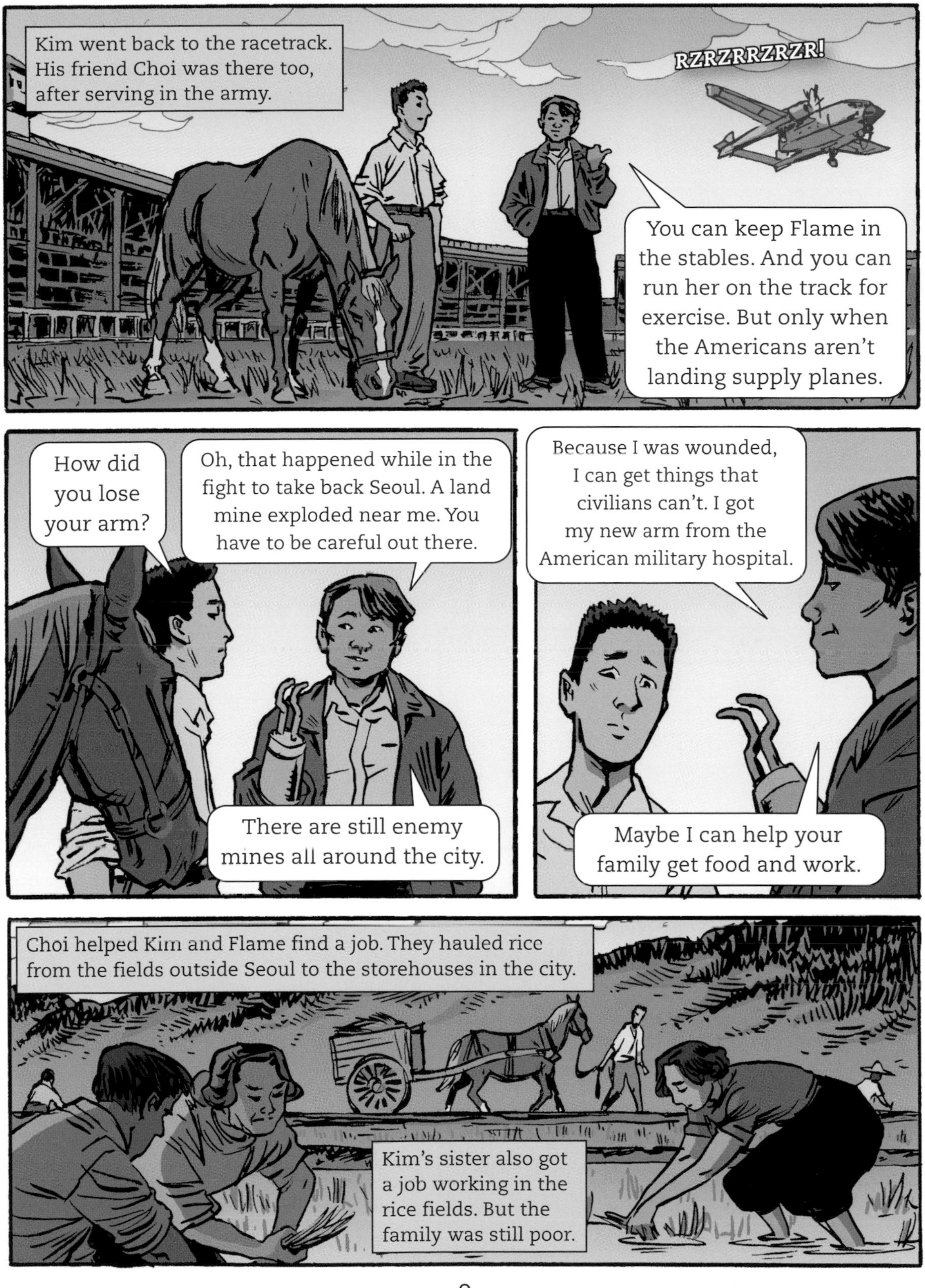
Kim went back to the racetrack. His friend Choi was there too, after serving in the army.
RZRZRRZRZR!
You can keep Flame in the stables. And you can run her on the track for exercise. But only when the Americans aren't landing supply planes.
How did you lose your arm?
Oh, that happened while in the fight to take back Seoul. A land mine exploded near me. You have to be careful out there.
There are still enemy mines all around the city.
Because I was wounded, I can get things that civilians can't. I got my new arm from the American military hospital.
Maybe I can help your family get food and work.
Choi helped Kim and Flame find a job. They hauled rice from the fields outside Seoul to the storehouses in the city.
Kim's sister also got a job working in the rice fields. But the family was still poor.

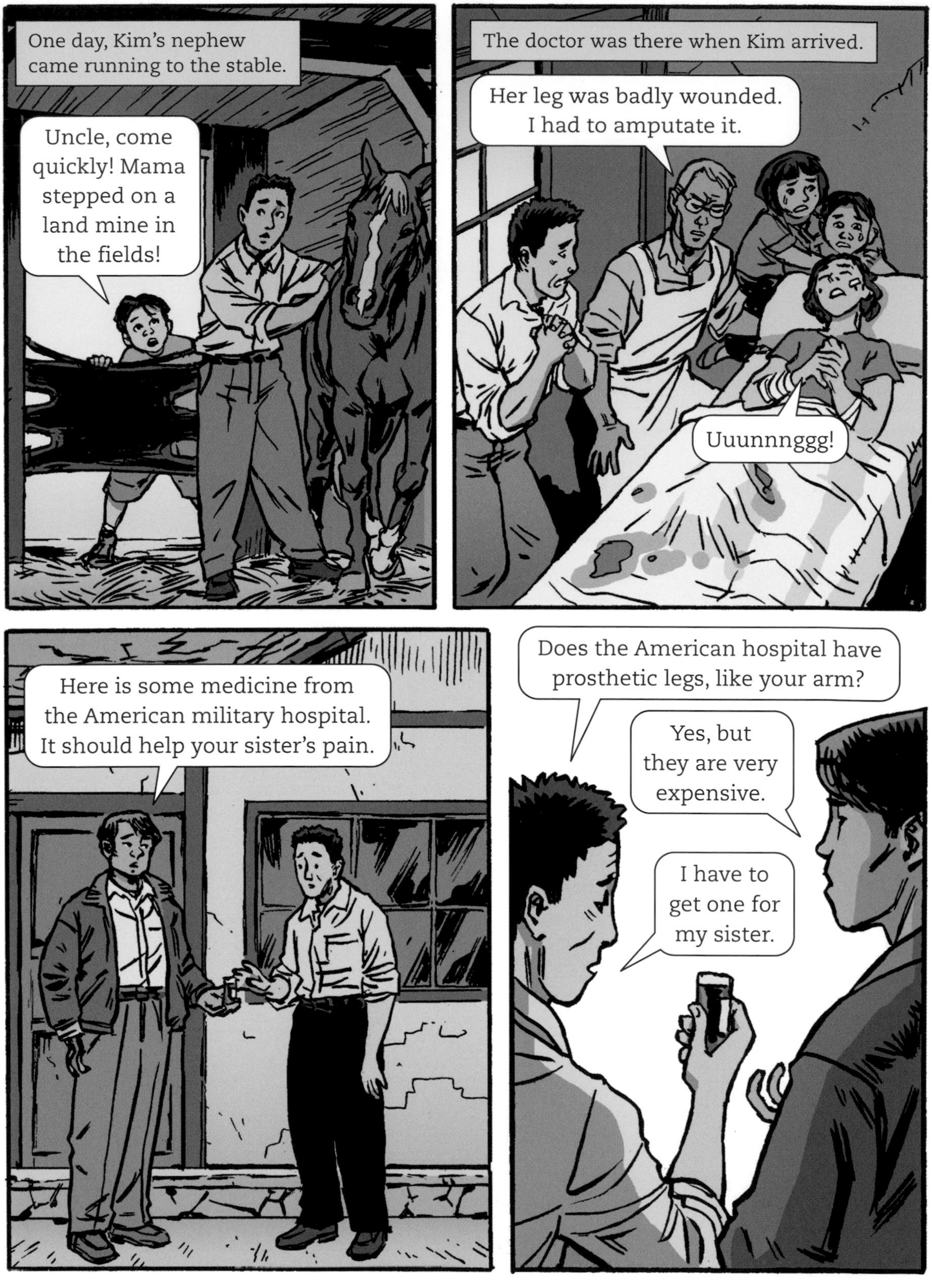

One day, Kim's nephew came running to the stable.
Uncle, come quickly! Mama stepped on a land mine in the fields!
The doctor was there when Kim arrived.
Her leg was badly wounded. I had to amputate it.
Uuunnnggg!
Here is some medicine from the American military hospital. It should help your sister's pain.
Does the American hospital have prosthetic legs, like your arm?
Yes, but they are very expensive.
I have to get one for my sister.

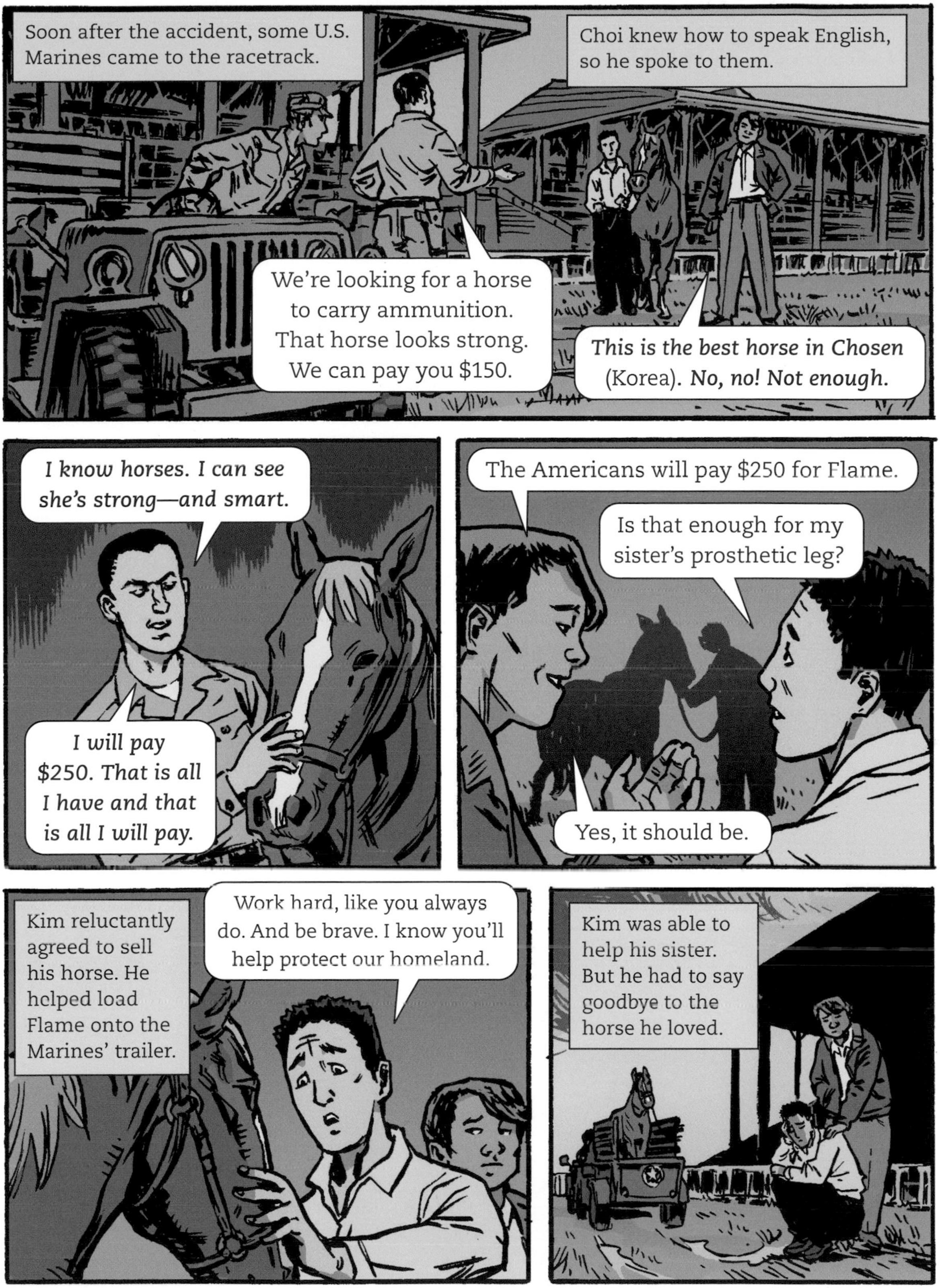
Soon after the accident, some U.S. Marines came to the racetrack.
Choi knew how to speak English, so he spoke to them.
We're looking for a horse to carry ammunition. That horse looks strong. We can pay you $150.
This is the best horse in Chosen (Korea). *No, no! Not enough.*
I know horses. I can see she's strong—and smart.
I will pay $250. That is all I have and that is all I will pay.
The Americans will pay $250 for Flame.
Is that enough for my sister's prosthetic leg?
Yes, it should be.
Kim reluctantly agreed to sell his horse. He helped load Flame onto the Marines' trailer.
Work hard, like you always do. And be brave. I know you'll help protect our homeland.
Kim was able to help his sister. But he had to say goodbye to the horse he loved.

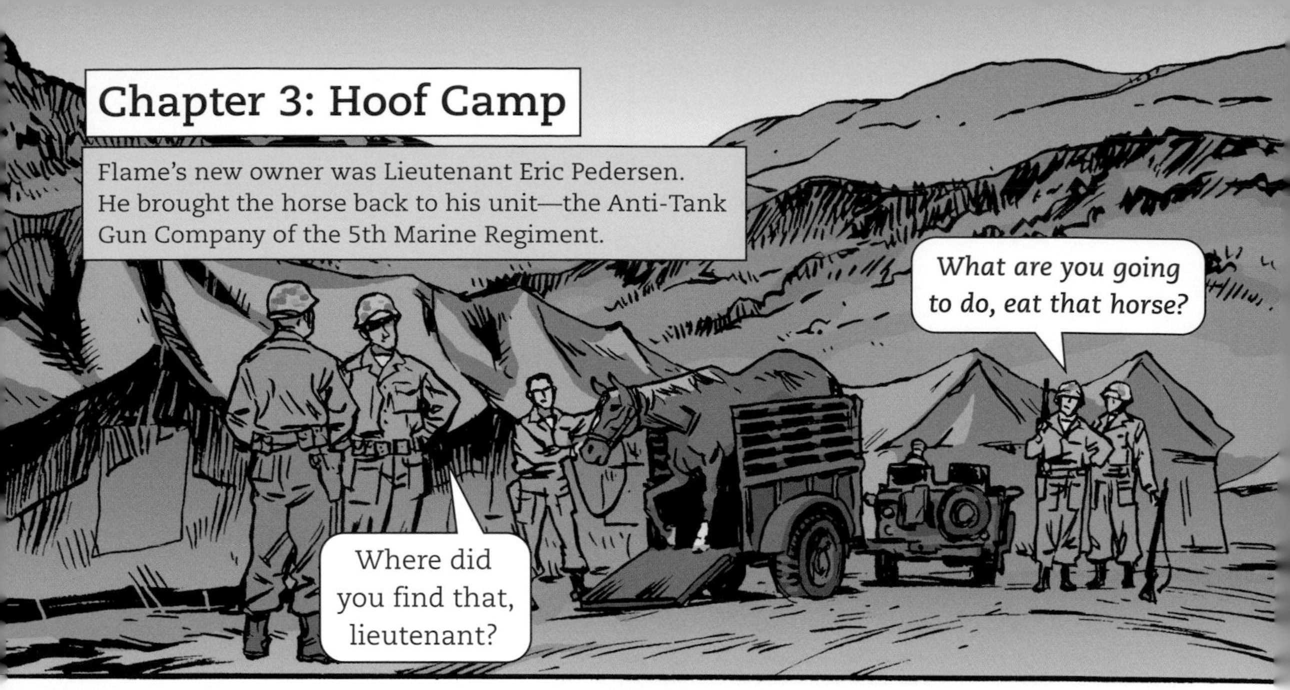
Chapter 3: Hoof Camp
Flame's new owner was Lieutenant Eric Pedersen. He brought the horse back to his unit—the Anti-Tank Gun Company of the 5th Marine Regiment.
Where did you find that, lieutenant?
What are you going to do, eat that horse?

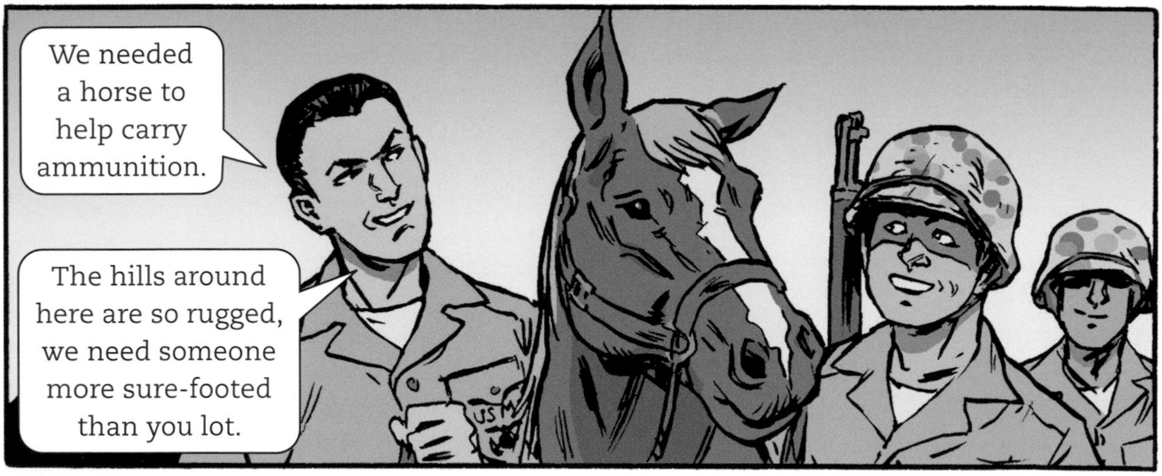
We needed a horse to help carry ammunition.
The hills around here are so rugged, we need someone more sure-footed than you lot.

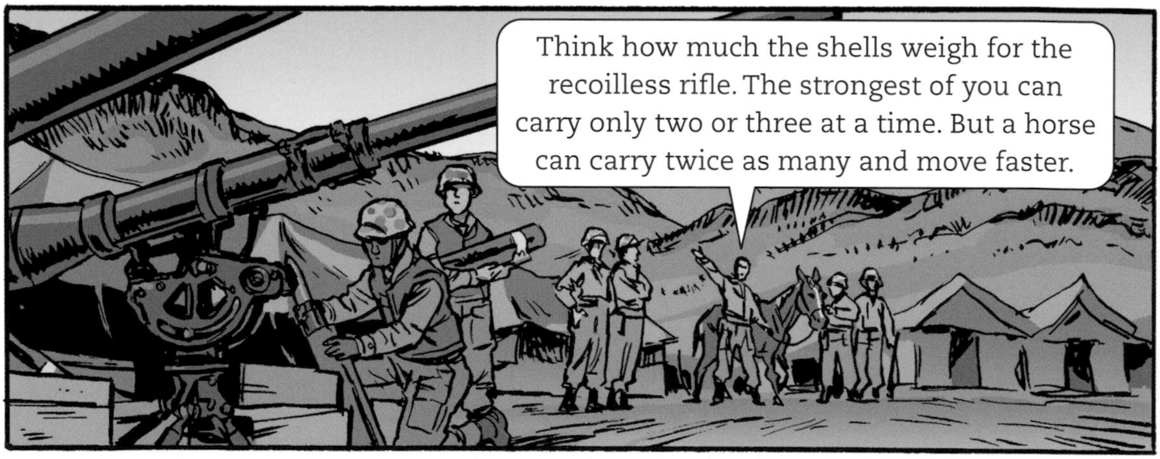
Think how much the shells weigh for the recoilless rifle. The strongest of you can carry only two or three at a time. But a horse can carry twice as many and move faster.

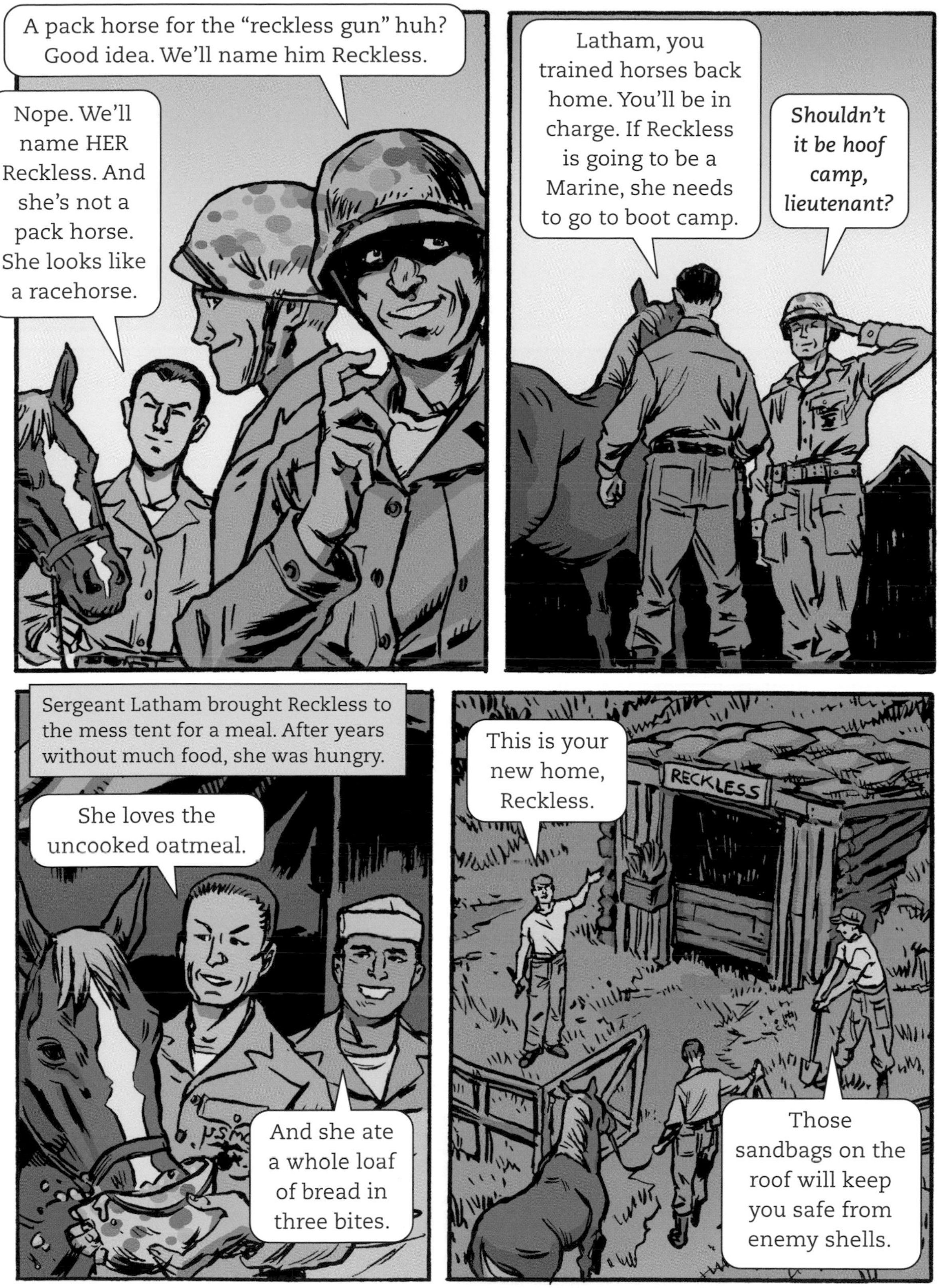
A pack horse for the "reckless gun" huh? Good idea. We'll name him Reckless.
Nope. We'll name HER Reckless. And she's not a pack horse. She looks like a racehorse.
Latham, you trained horses back home. You'll be in charge. If Reckless is going to be a Marine, she needs to go to boot camp.
Shouldn't it be hoof camp, lieutenant?
Sergeant Latham brought Reckless to the mess tent for a meal. After years without much food, she was hungry.
She loves the uncooked oatmeal.
And she ate a whole loaf of bread in three bites.
This is your new home, Reckless.
RECKLESS
Those sandbags on the roof will keep you safe from enemy shells.

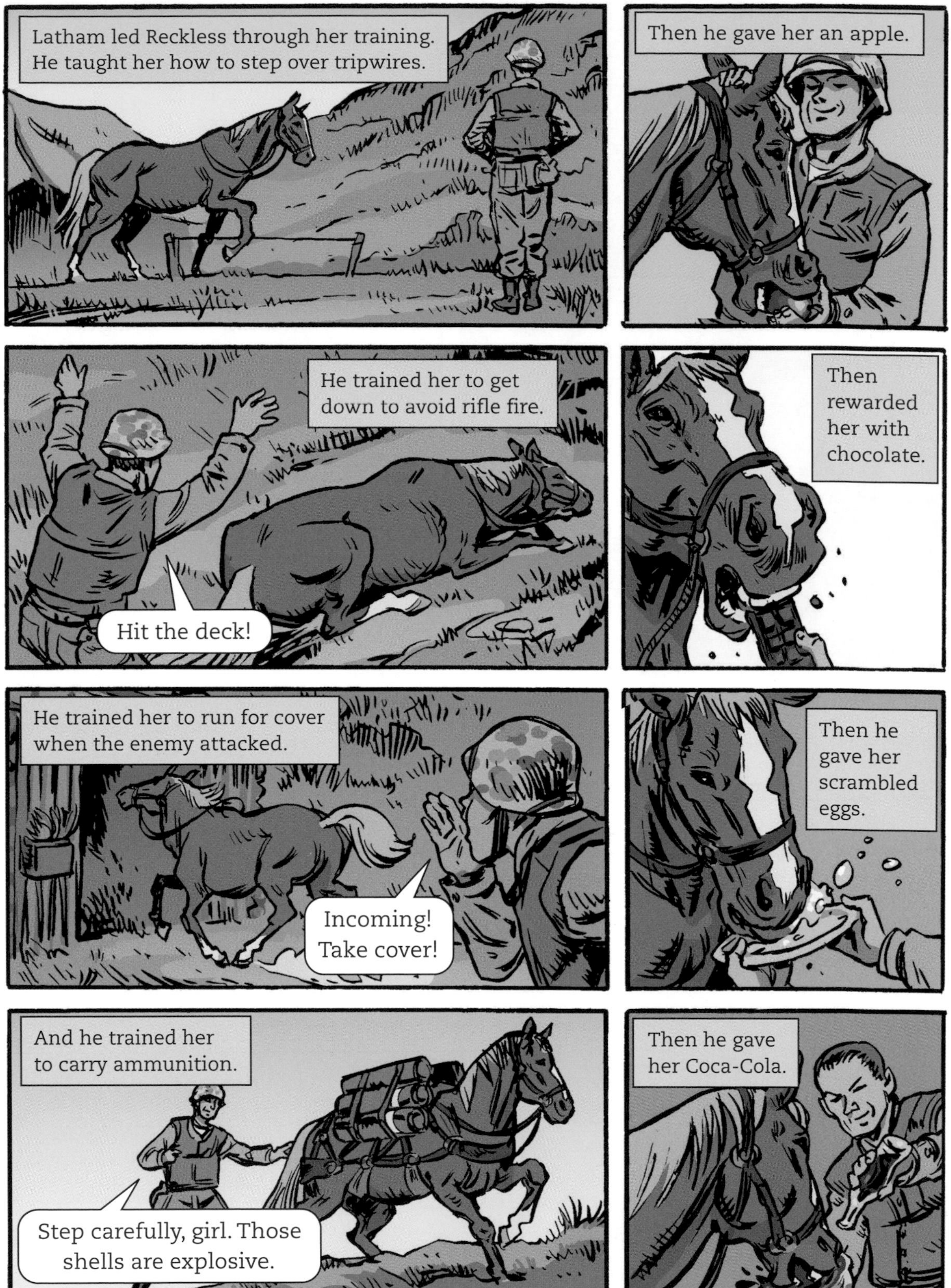
Latham led Reckless through her training. He taught her how to step over tripwires.
Then he gave her an apple.
He trained her to get down to avoid rifle fire.
Hit the deck!
Then rewarded her with chocolate.
He trained her to run for cover when the enemy attacked.
Incoming! Take cover!
Then he gave her scrambled eggs.
And he trained her to carry ammunition.
Step carefully, girl. Those shells are explosive.
Then he gave her Coca-Cola.

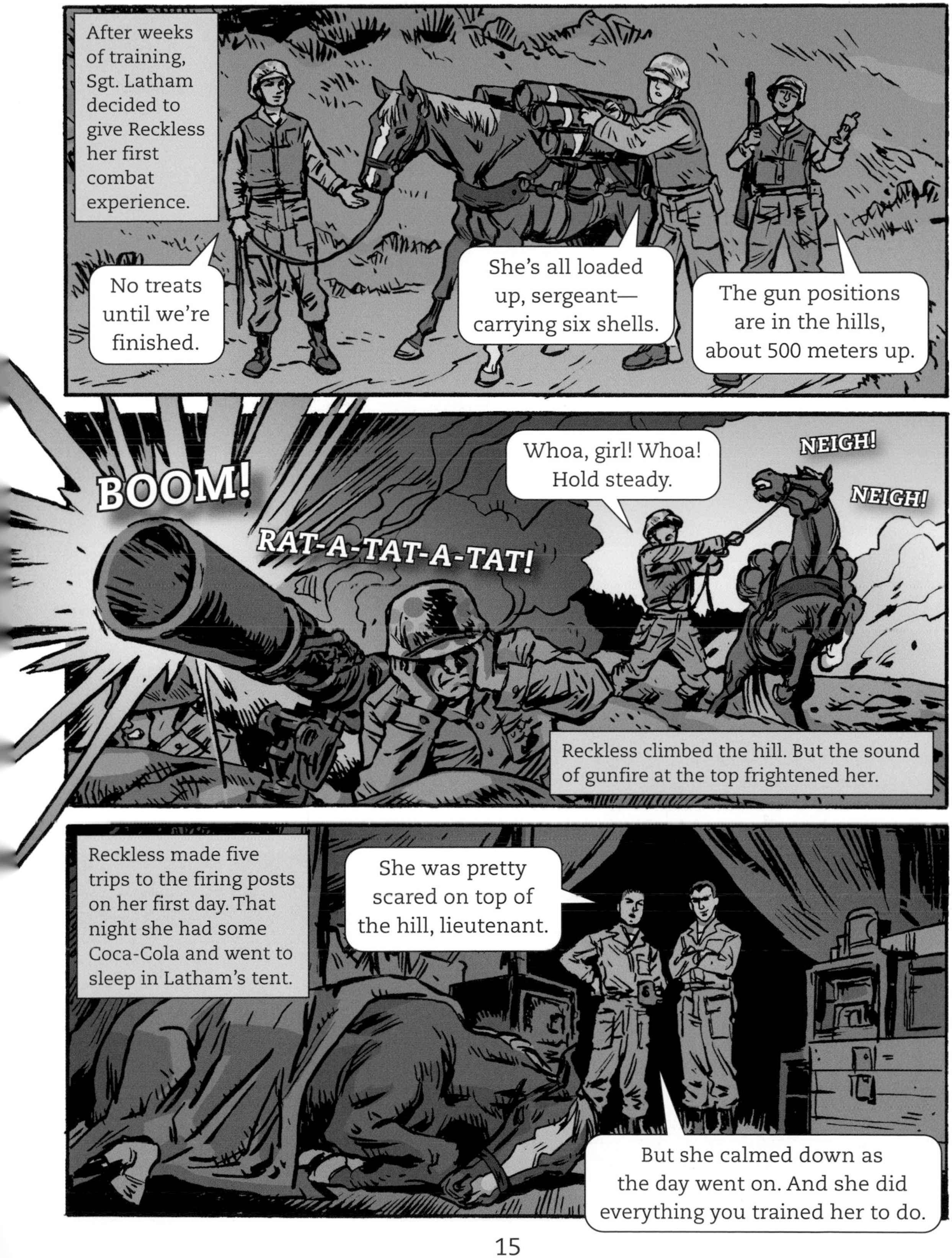
After weeks of training, Sgt. Latham decided to give Reckless her first combat experience.
No treats until we're finished.
She's all loaded up, sergeant—carrying six shells.
The gun positions are in the hills, about 500 meters up.
BOOM!
RAT-A-TAT-A-TAT!
Whoa, girl! Whoa! Hold steady.
NEIGH!
NEIGH!
Reckless climbed the hill. But the sound of gunfire at the top frightened her.
Reckless made five trips to the firing posts on her first day. That night she had some Coca-Cola and went to sleep in Latham's tent.
She was pretty scared on top of the hill, lieutenant.
But she calmed down as the day went on. And she did everything you trained her to do.

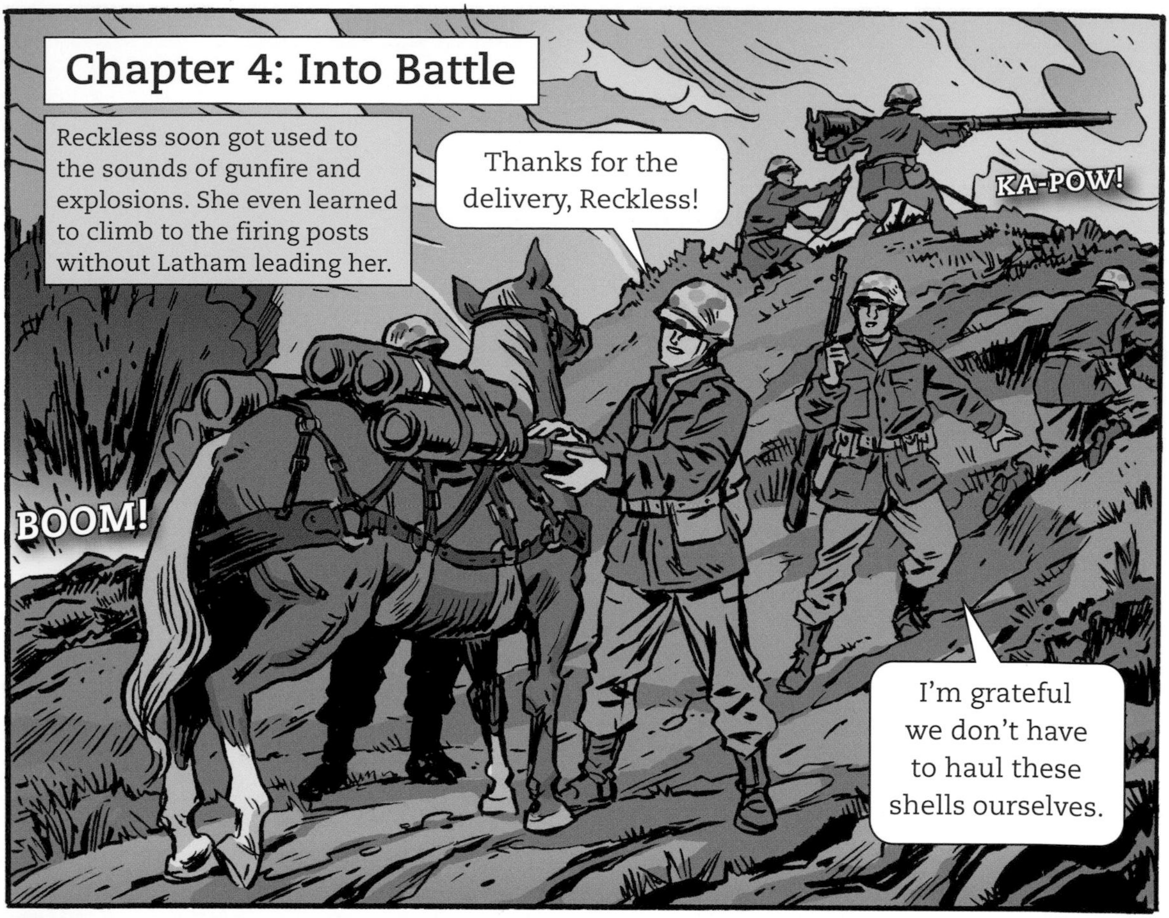
Chapter 4: Into Battle
Reckless soon got used to the sounds of gunfire and explosions. She even learned to climb to the firing posts without Latham leading her.
Thanks for the delivery, Reckless!
KA-POW!
BOOM!
I'm grateful we don't have to haul these shells ourselves.

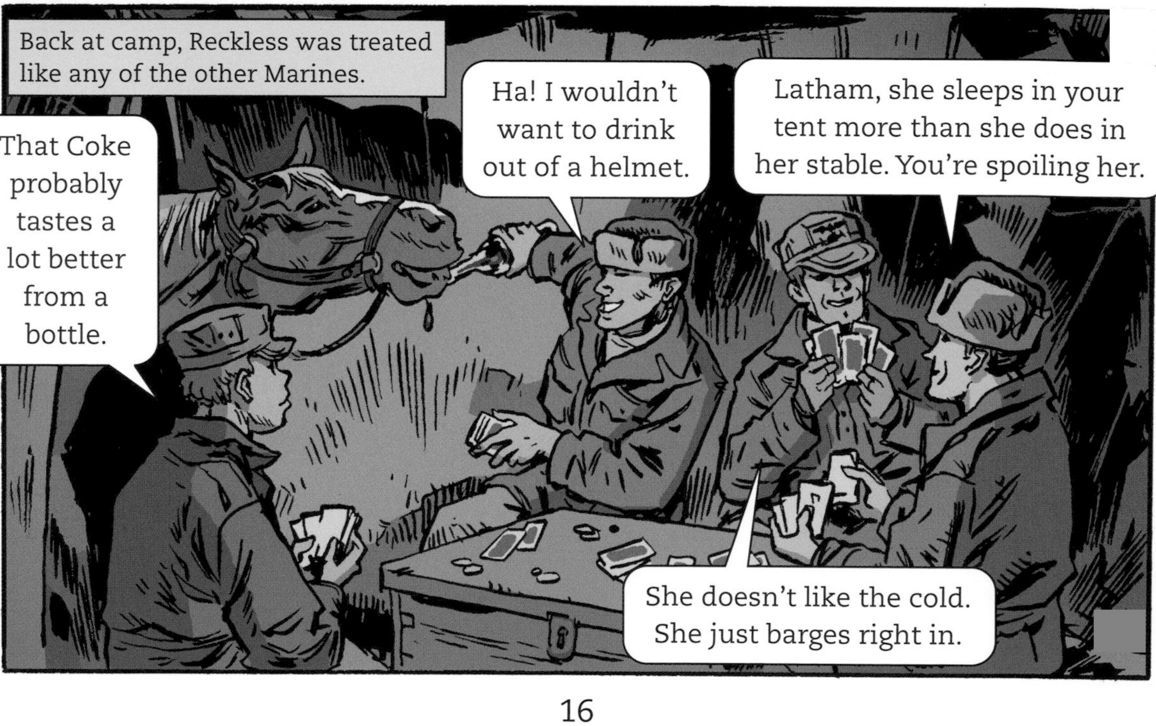
Back at camp, Reckless was treated like any of the other Marines.
That Coke probably tastes a lot better from a bottle.
Ha! I wouldn't want to drink out of a helmet.
Latham, she sleeps in your tent more than she does in her stable. You're spoiling her.
She doesn't like the cold. She just barges right in.

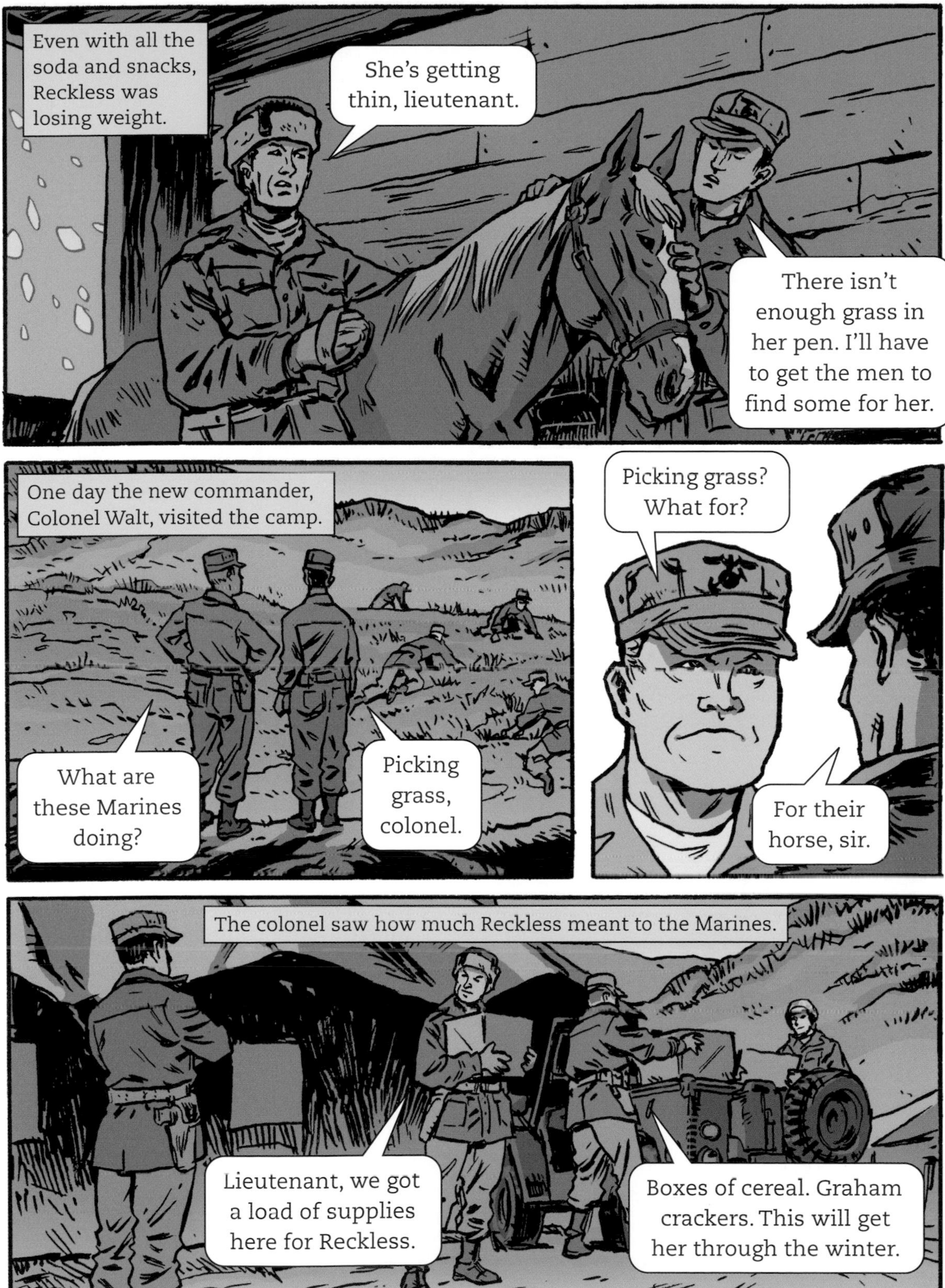
Even with all the soda and snacks, Reckless was losing weight.
She's getting thin, lieutenant.
There isn't enough grass in her pen. I'll have to get the men to find some for her.
One day the new commander, Colonel Walt, visited the camp.
What are these Marines doing?
Picking grass, colonel.
Picking grass? What for?
For their horse, sir.
The colonel saw how much Reckless meant to the Marines.
Lieutenant, we got a load of supplies here for Reckless.
Boxes of cereal. Graham crackers. This will get her through the winter.

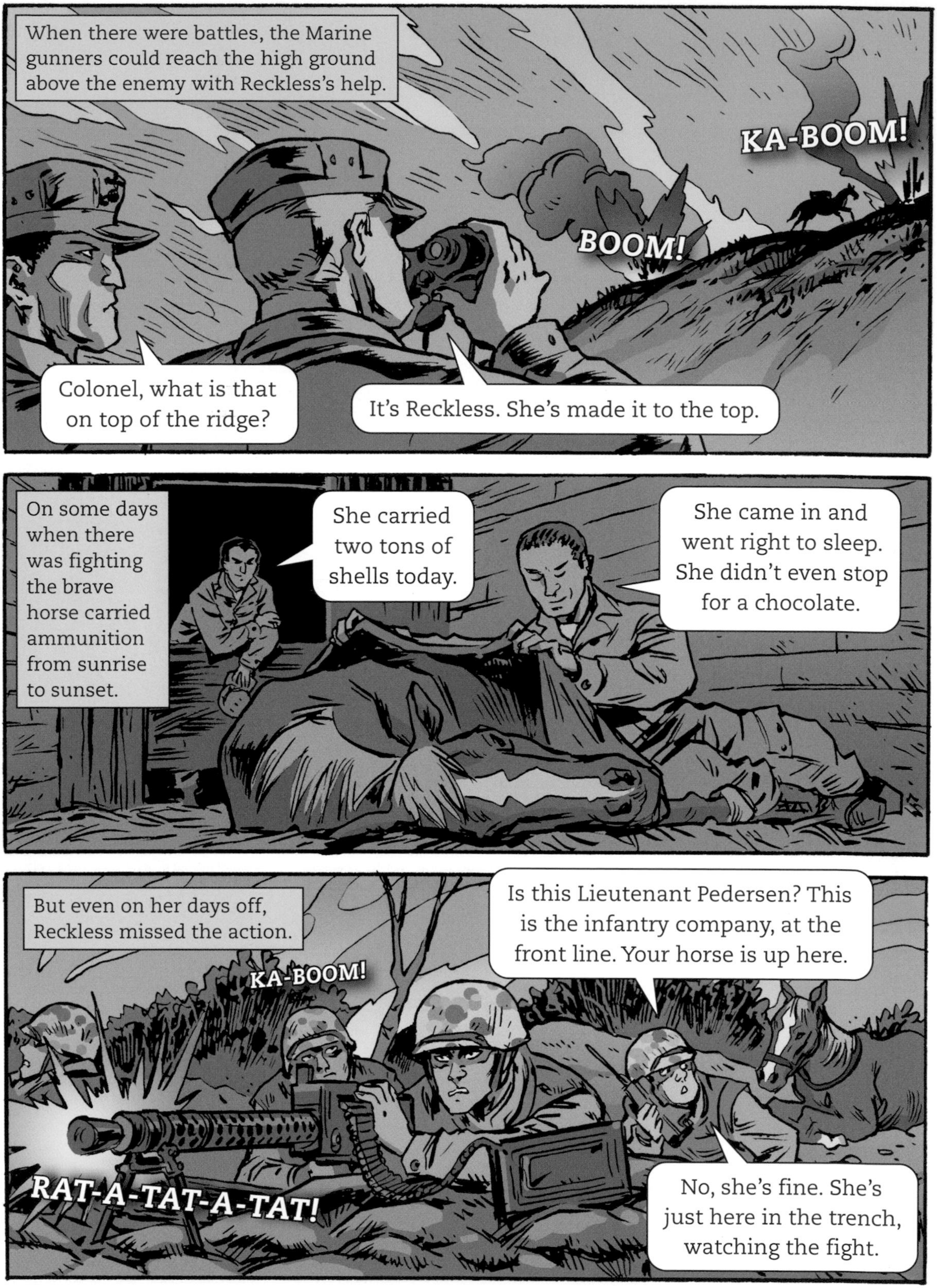

When there were battles, the Marine gunners could reach the high ground above the enemy with Reckless's help.
KA-BOOM!
BOOM!
Colonel, what is that on top of the ridge?
It's Reckless. She's made it to the top.
On some days when there was fighting the brave horse carried ammunition from sunrise to sunset.
She carried two tons of shells today.
She came in and went right to sleep. She didn't even stop for a chocolate.
But even on her days off, Reckless missed the action.
KA-BOOM!
Is this Lieutenant Pedersen? This is the infantry company, at the front line. Your horse is up here.
RAT-A-TAT-A-TAT!
No, she's fine. She's just here in the trench, watching the fight.

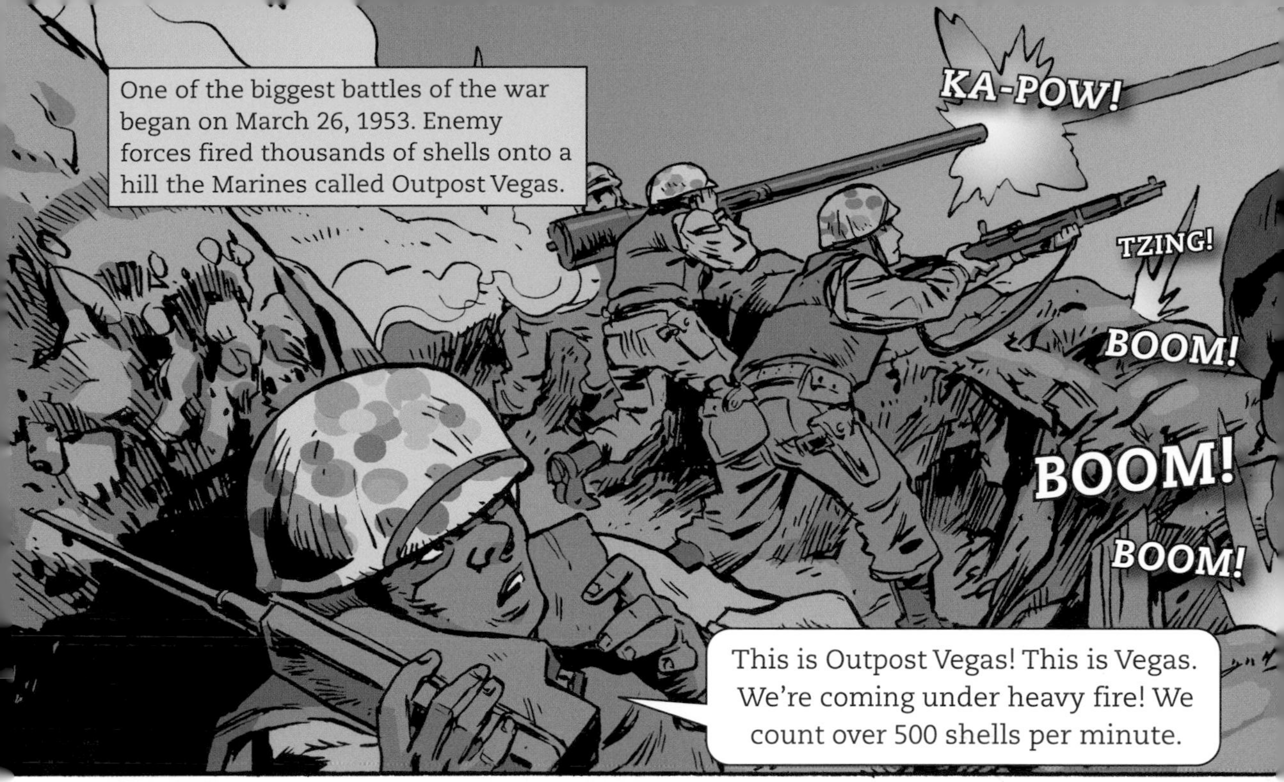
One of the biggest battles of the war began on March 26, 1953. Enemy forces fired thousands of shells onto a hill the Marines called Outpost Vegas.
KA-POW!
TZING!
BOOM!
BOOM!
BOOM!
This is Outpost Vegas! This is Vegas. We're coming under heavy fire! We count over 500 shells per minute.

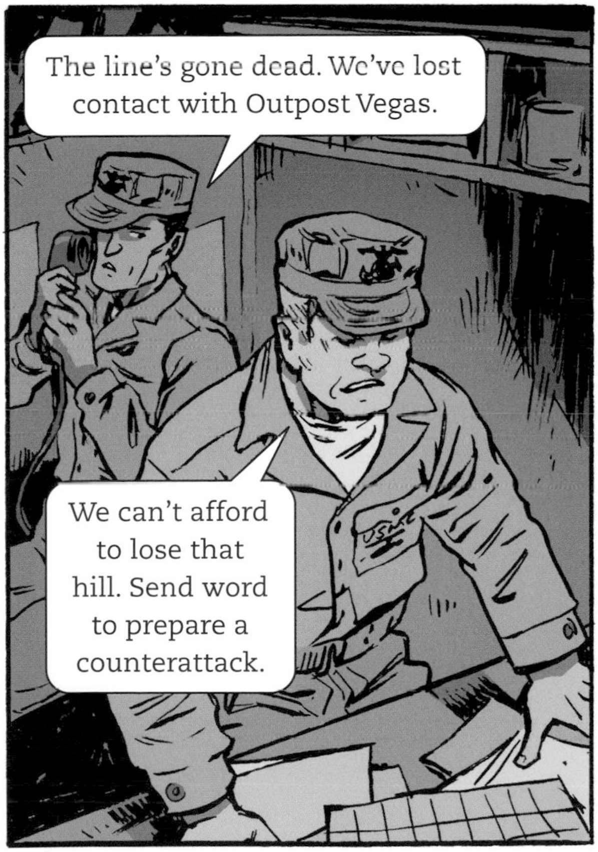
The line's gone dead. We've lost contact with Outpost Vegas.
We can't afford to lose that hill. Send word to prepare a counterattack.

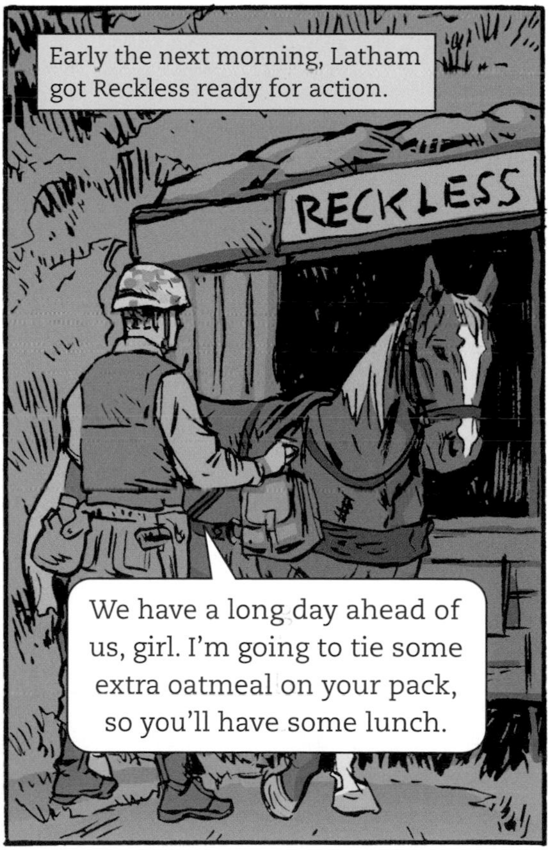
Early the next morning, Latham got Reckless ready for action.
RECKLESS
We have a long day ahead of us, girl. I'm going to tie some extra oatmeal on your pack, so you'll have some lunch.

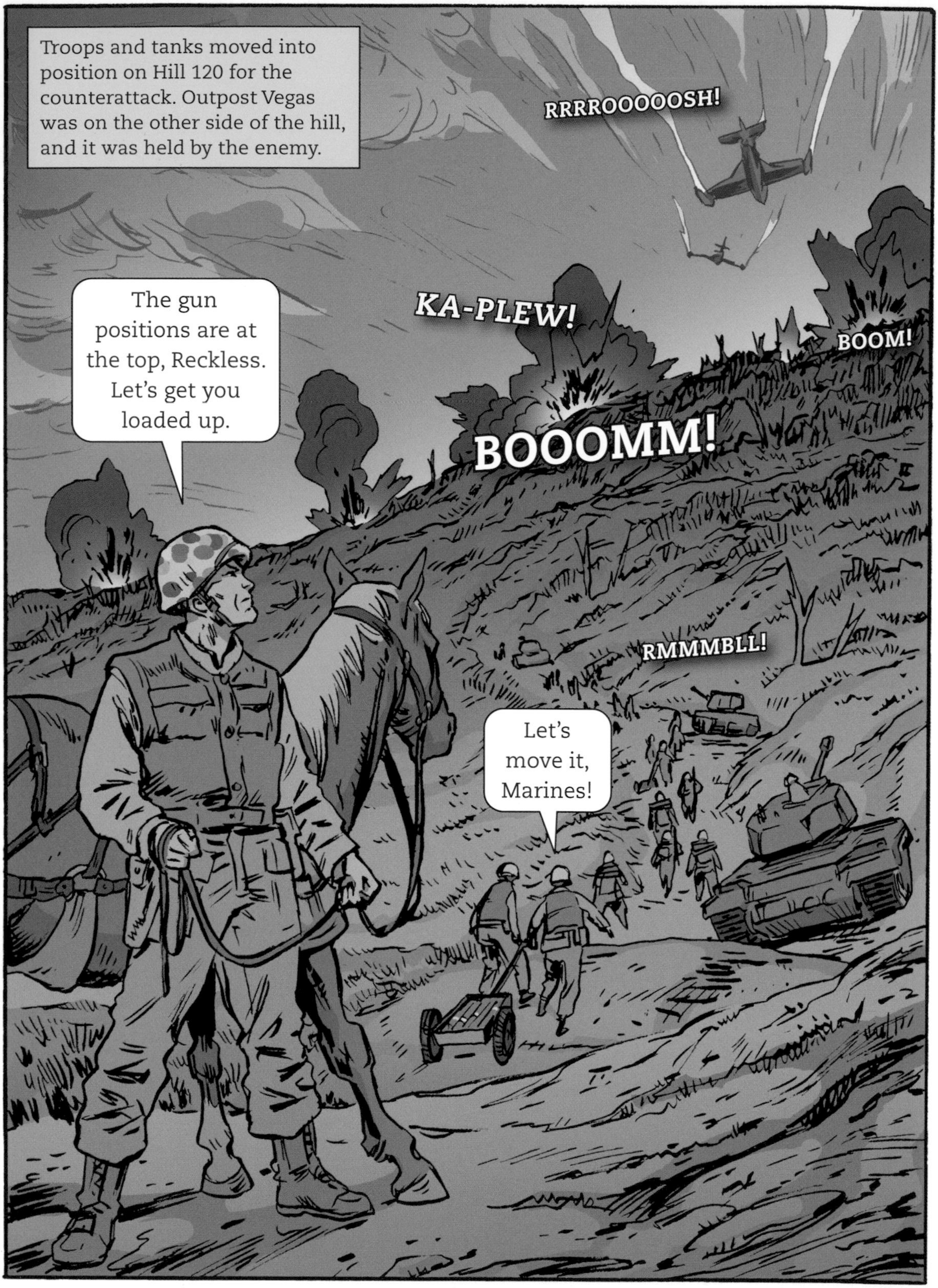
Troops and tanks moved into position on Hill 120 for the counterattack. Outpost Vegas was on the other side of the hill, and it was held by the enemy.
RRRROOOOOOSH!
The gun positions are at the top, Reckless. Let's get you loaded up.
KA-PLEW!
BOOM!
BOOOMM!
RMMMBLL!
Let's move it, Marines!

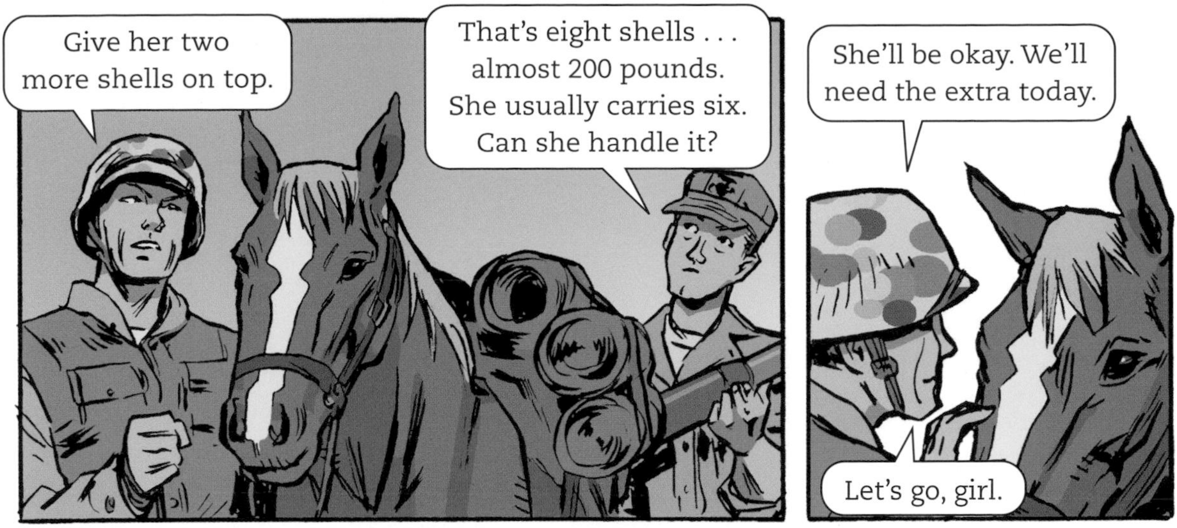
Give her two more shells on top.
That's eight shells . . . almost 200 pounds. She usually carries six. Can she handle it?
She'll be okay. We'll need the extra today.
Let's go, girl.

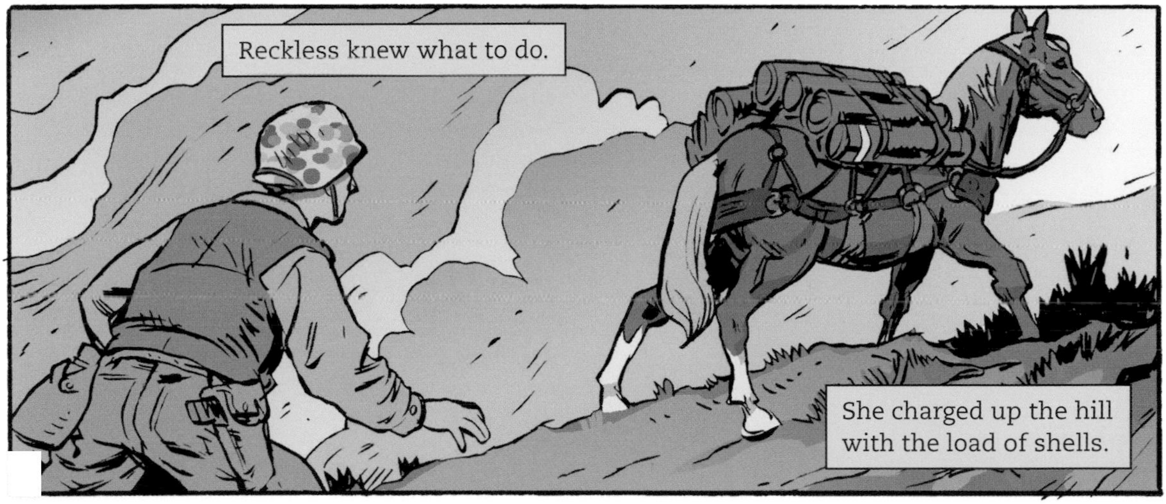
Reckless knew what to do.
She charged up the hill with the load of shells.

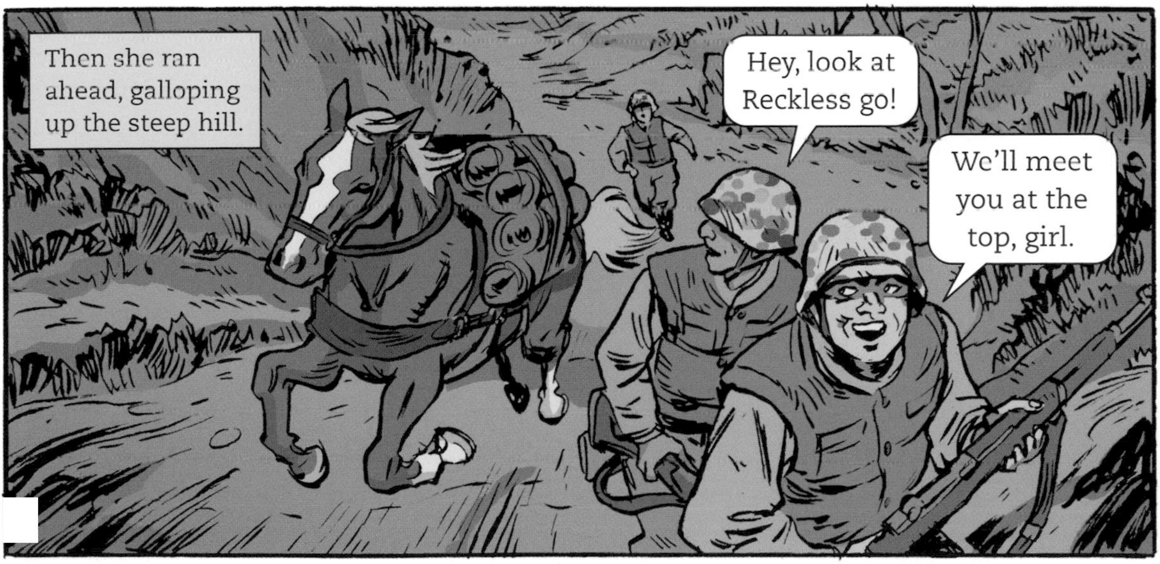
Then she ran ahead, galloping up the steep hill.
Hey, look at Reckless go!
We'll meet you at the top, girl.

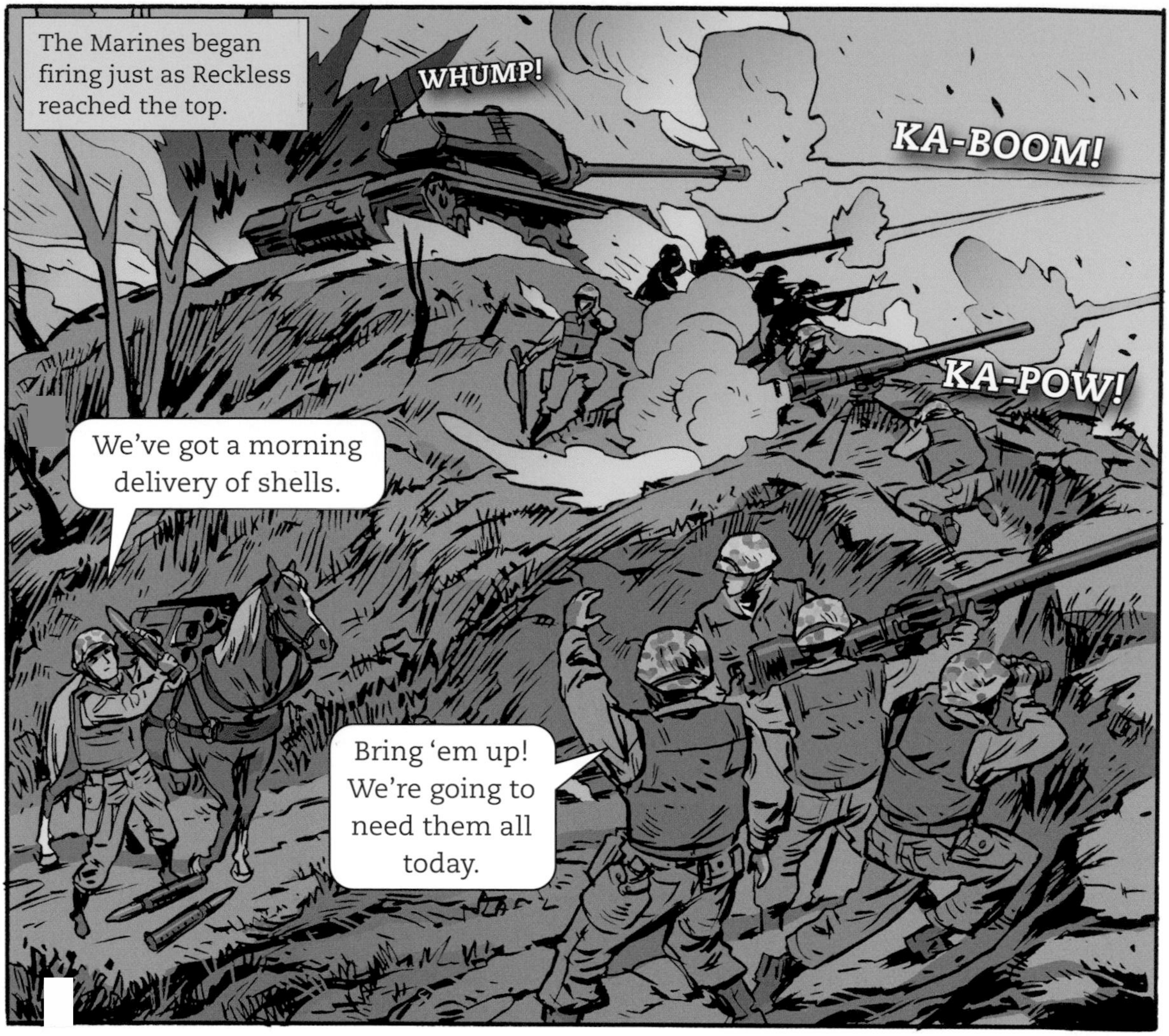

The Marines began firing just as Reckless reached the top.
WHUMP!
KA-BOOM!
KA-POW!
We've got a morning delivery of shells.
Bring 'em up! We're going to need them all today.

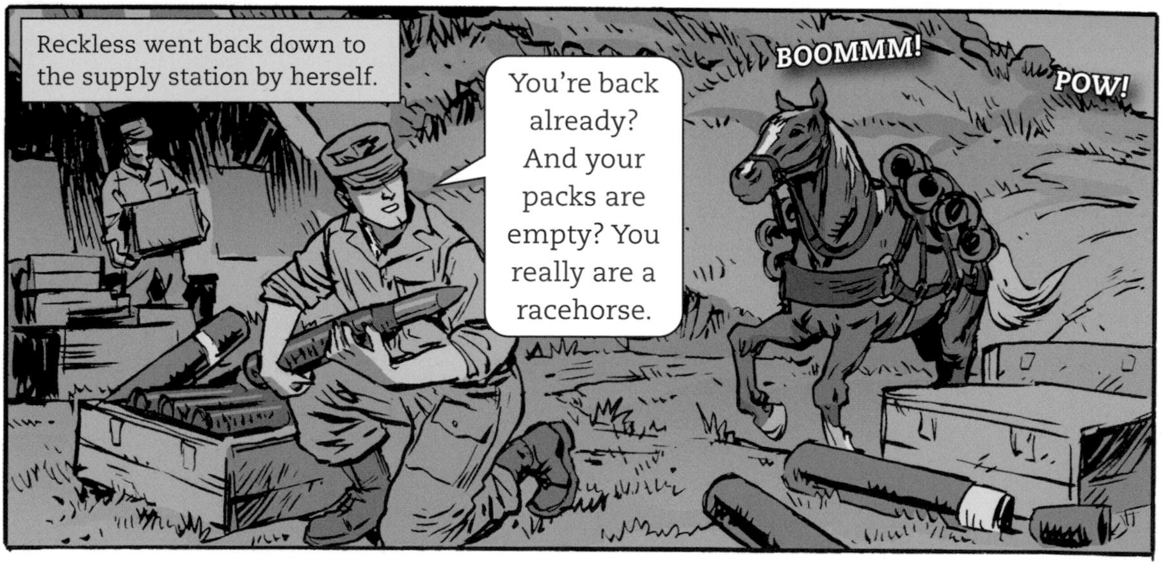

Reckless went back down to the supply station by herself.
BOOMMM!
POW!
You're back already? And your packs are empty? You really are a racehorse.

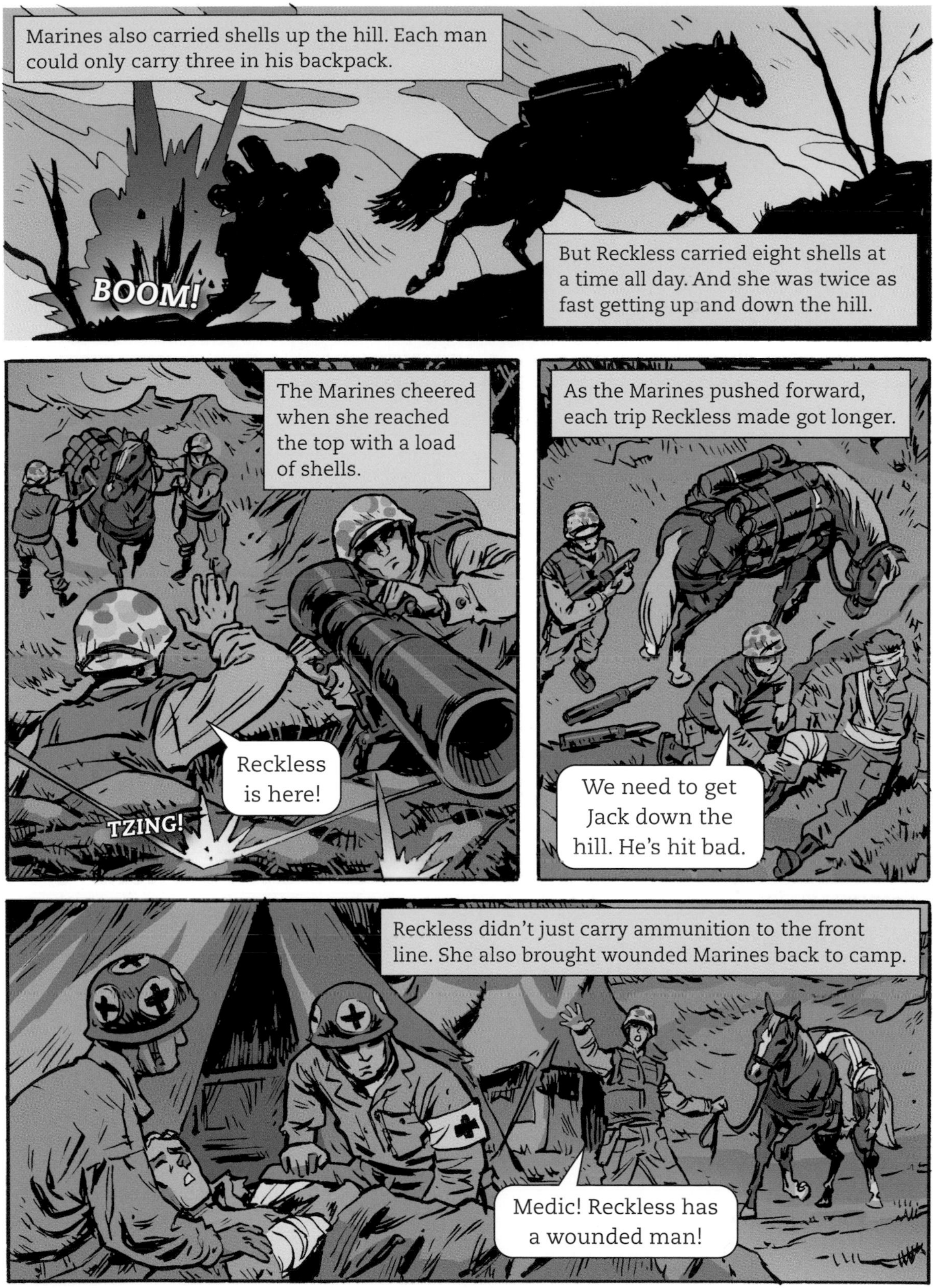
Marines also carried shells up the hill. Each man could only carry three in his backpack.
BOOM!
But Reckless carried eight shells at a time all day. And she was twice as fast getting up and down the hill.
The Marines cheered when she reached the top with a load of shells.
Reckless is here!
TZING!
As the Marines pushed forward, each trip Reckless made got longer.
We need to get Jack down the hill. He's hit bad.
Reckless didn't just carry ammunition to the front line. She also brought wounded Marines back to camp.
Medic! Reckless has a wounded man!

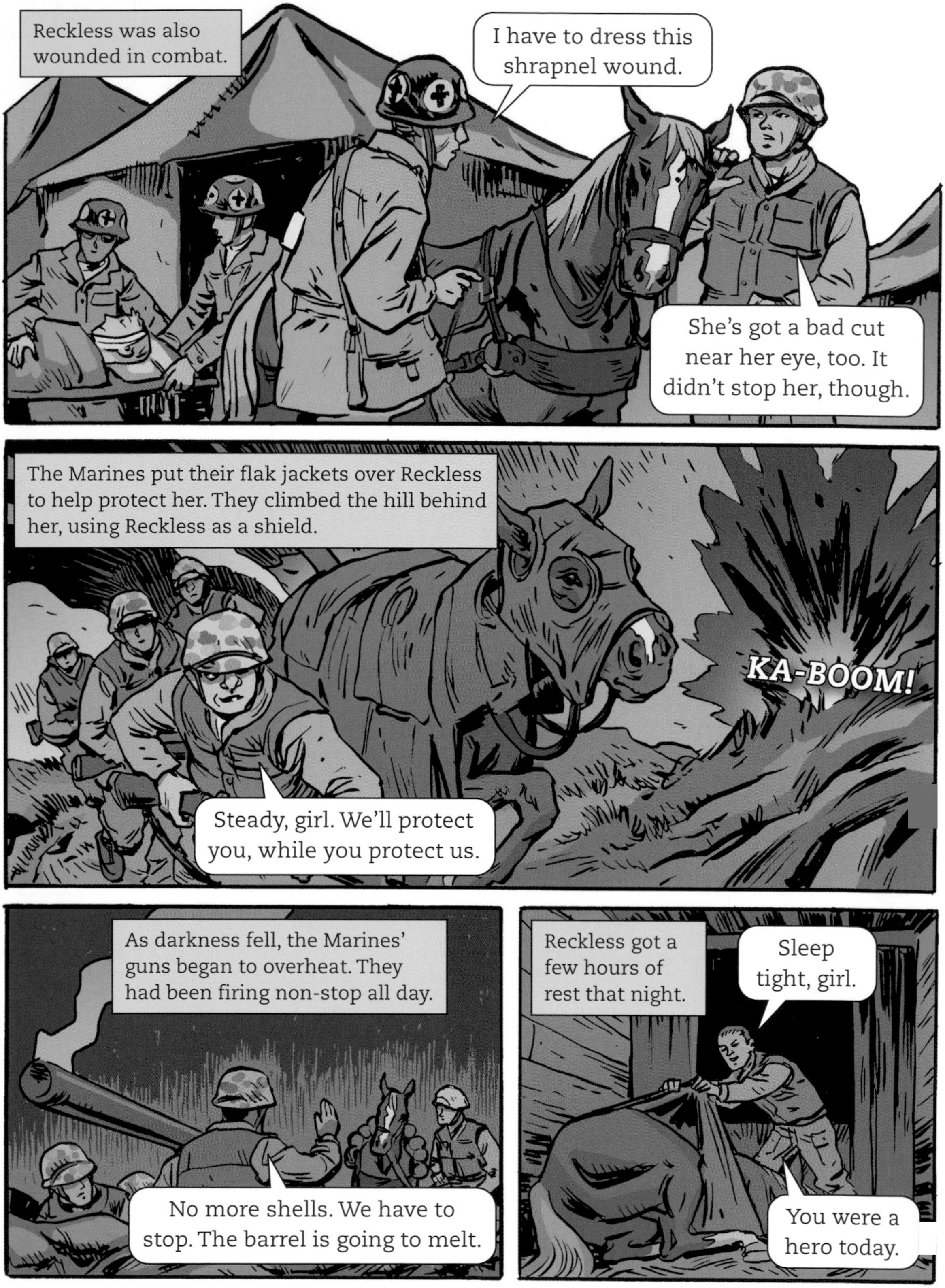
Reckless was also wounded in combat.
I have to dress this shrapnel wound.
She's got a bad cut near her eye, too. It didn't stop her, though.
The Marines put their flak jackets over Reckless to help protect her. They climbed the hill behind her, using Reckless as a shield.
KA-BOOM!
Steady, girl. We'll protect you, while you protect us.
As darkness fell, the Marines' guns began to overheat. They had been firing non-stop all day.
No more shells. We have to stop. The barrel is going to melt.
Reckless got a few hours of rest that night.
Sleep tight, girl.
You were a hero today.

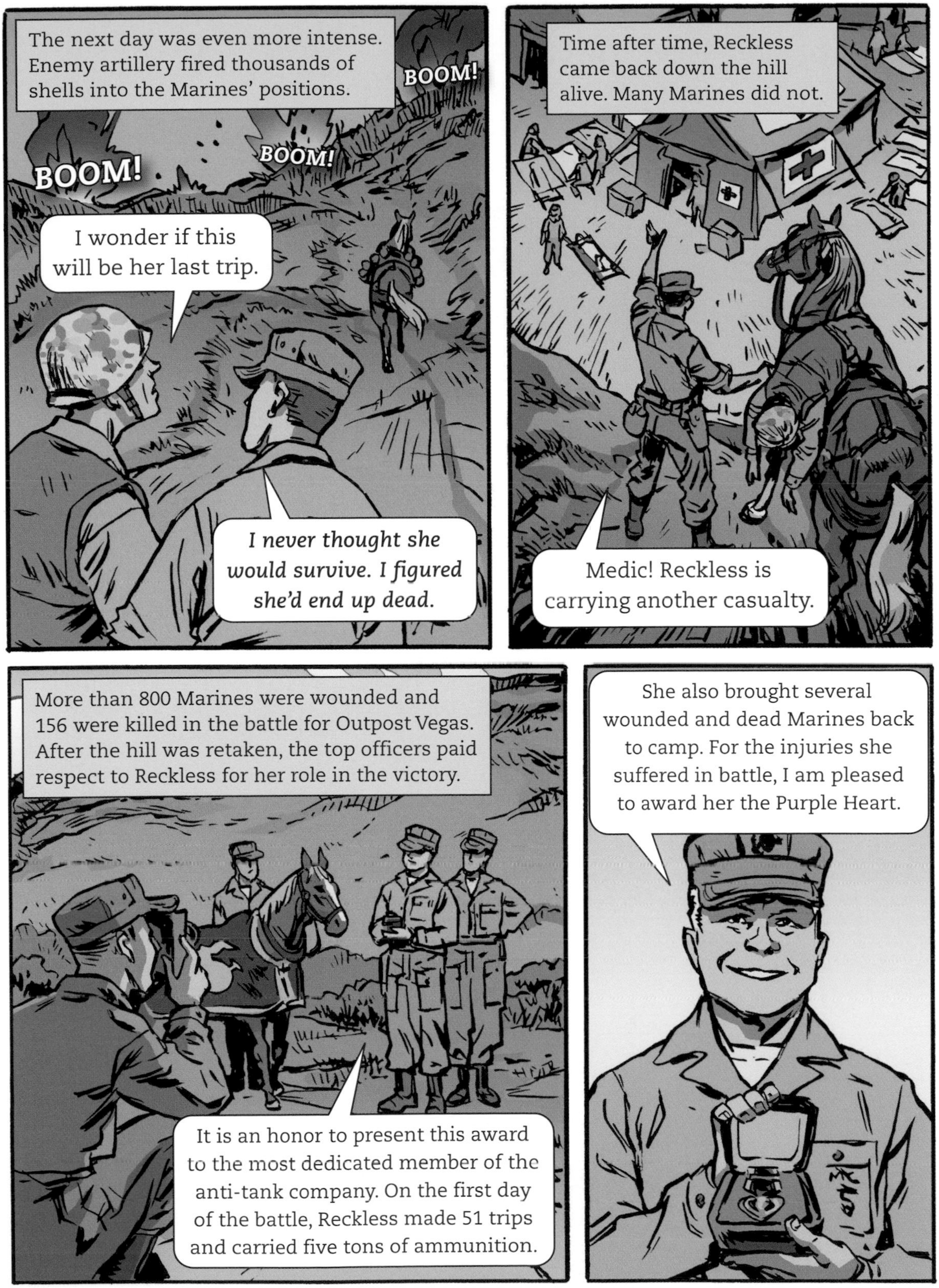
The next day was even more intense. Enemy artillery fired thousands of shells into the Marines' positions.
BOOM!
BOOM!
BOOM!
I wonder if this will be her last trip.
I never thought she would survive. I figured she'd end up dead.
Time after time, Reckless came back down the hill alive. Many Marines did not.
Medic! Reckless is carrying another casualty.
More than 800 Marines were wounded and 156 were killed in the battle for Outpost Vegas. After the hill was retaken, the top officers paid respect to Reckless for her role in the victory.
It is an honor to present this award to the most dedicated member of the anti-tank company. On the first day of the battle, Reckless made 51 trips and carried five tons of ammunition.
She also brought several wounded and dead Marines back to camp. For the injuries she suffered in battle, I am pleased to award her the Purple Heart.

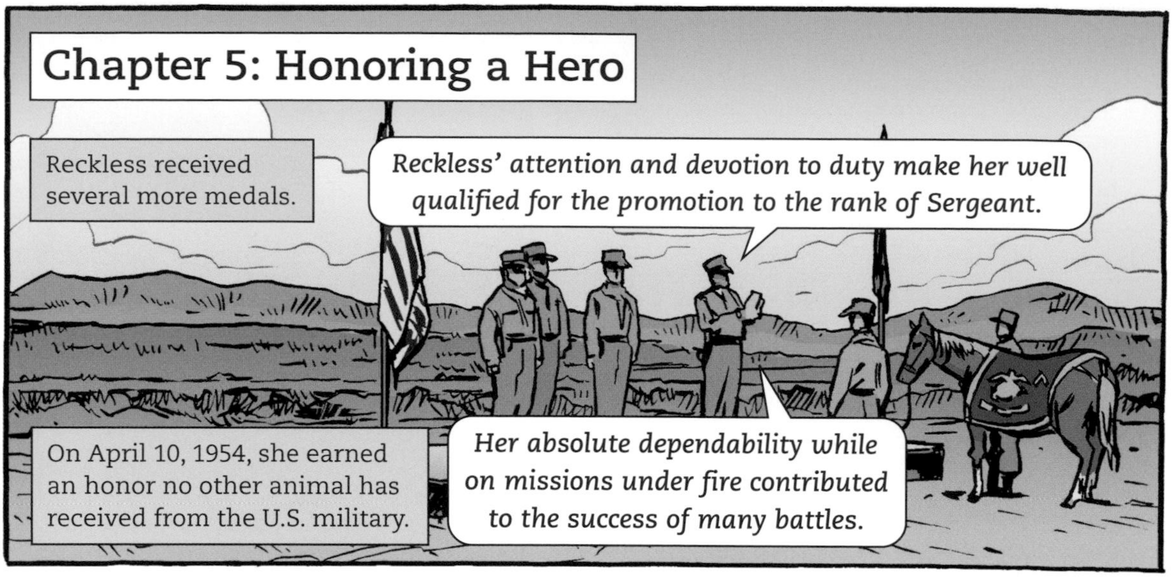
Chapter 5: Honoring a Hero
Reckless received several more medals.
Reckless' attention and devotion to duty make her well qualified for the promotion to the rank of Sergeant.
On April 10, 1954, she earned an honor no other animal has received from the U.S. military.
Her absolute dependability while on missions under fire contributed to the success of many battles.

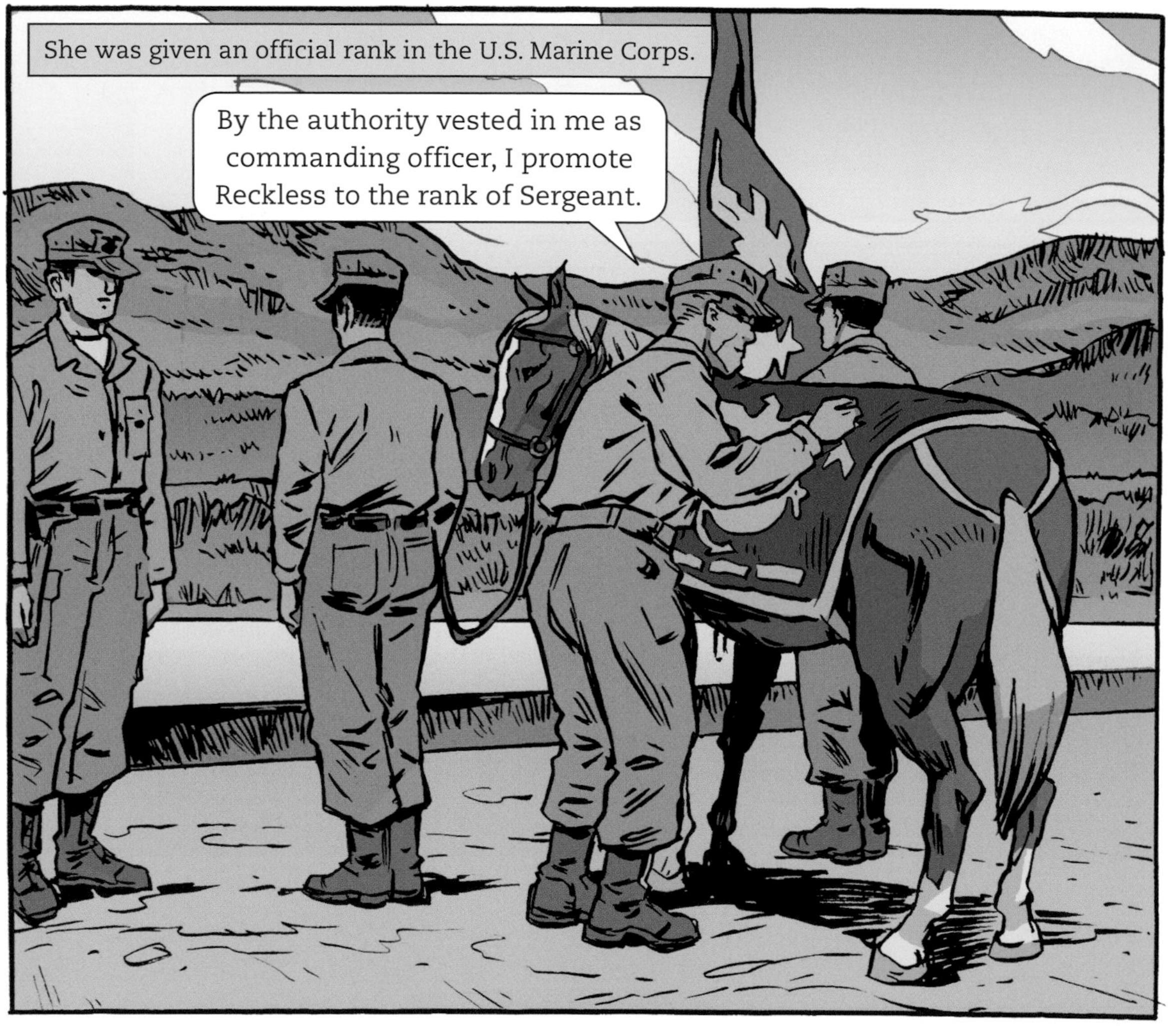
She was given an official rank in the U.S. Marine Corps.
By the authority vested in me as commanding officer, I promote Reckless to the rank of Sergeant.

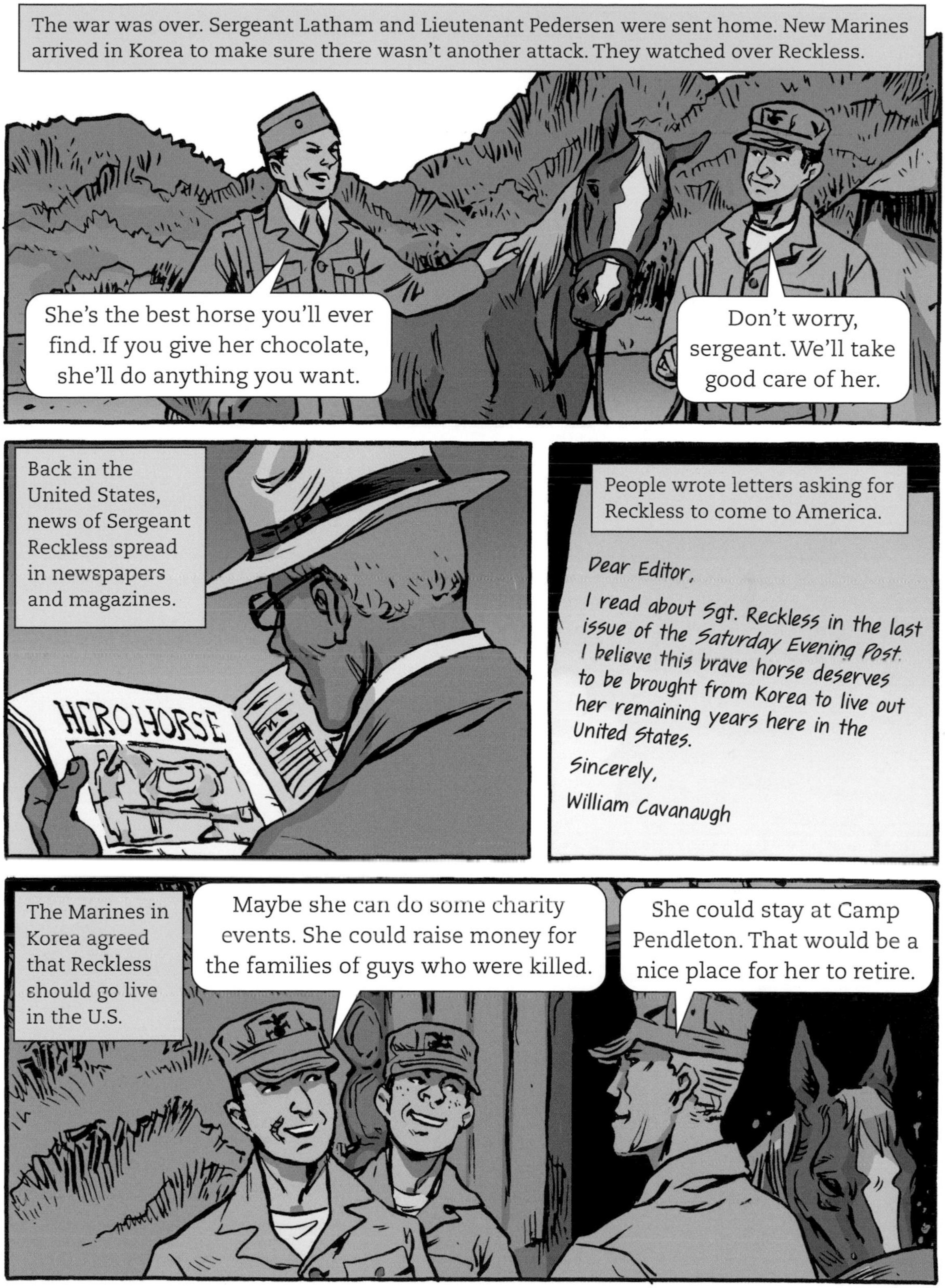
The war was over. Sergeant Latham and Lieutenant Pedersen were sent home. New Marines arrived in Korea to make sure there wasn't another attack. They watched over Reckless.
She's the best horse you'll ever find. If you give her chocolate, she'll do anything you want.
Don't worry, sergeant. We'll take good care of her.
Back in the United States, news of Sergeant Reckless spread in newspapers and magazines.
HERO HORSE
People wrote letters asking for Reckless to come to America.
Dear Editor,
I read about Sgt. Reckless in the last issue of the Saturday Evening Post. I believe this brave horse deserves to be brought from Korea to live out her remaining years here in the United States.
Sincerely,
William Cavanaugh
The Marines in Korea agreed that Reckless should go live in the U.S.
Maybe she can do some charity events. She could raise money for the families of guys who were killed.
She could stay at Camp Pendleton. That would be a nice place for her to retire.

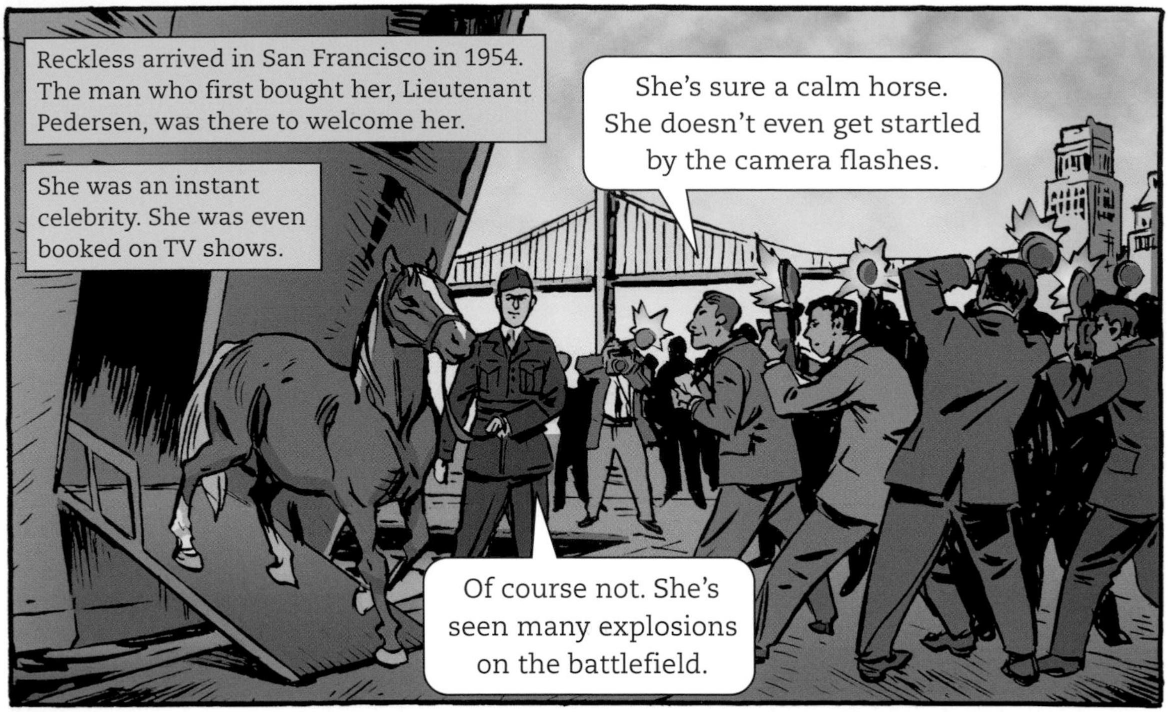
Reckless arrived in San Francisco in 1954. The man who first bought her, Lieutenant Pedersen, was there to welcome her.
She was an instant celebrity. She was even booked on TV shows.
She's sure a calm horse. She doesn't even get startled by the camera flashes.
Of course not. She's seen many explosions on the battlefield.

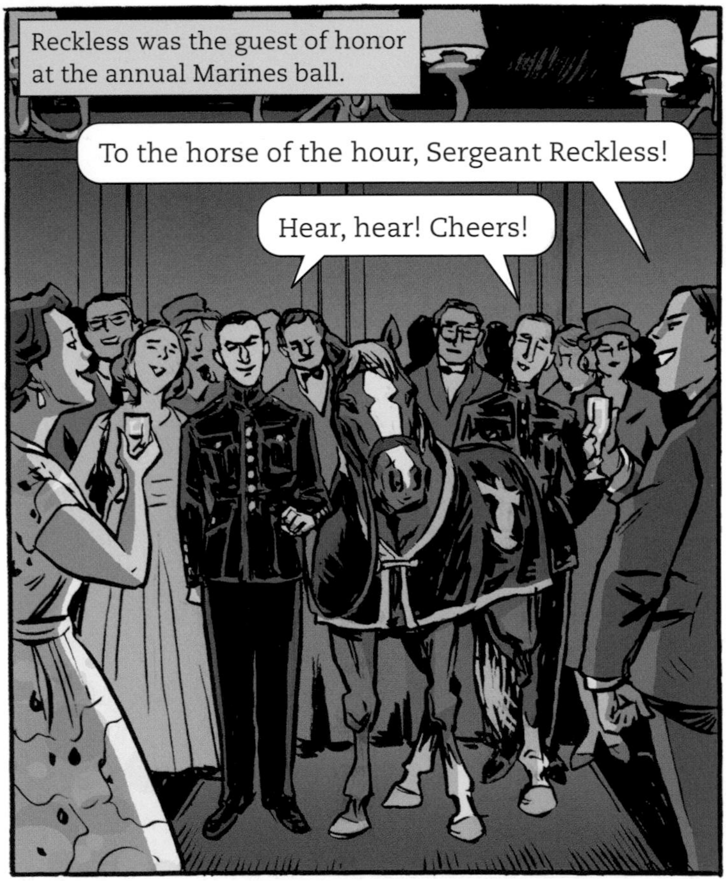
Reckless was the guest of honor at the annual Marines ball.
To the horse of the hour, Sergeant Reckless!
Hear, hear! Cheers!

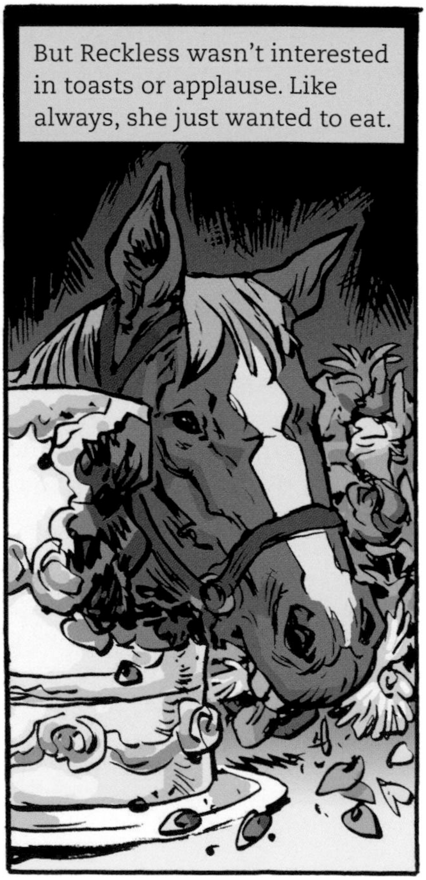
But Reckless wasn't interested in toasts or applause. Like always, she just wanted to eat.

Reckless After the War

After arriving in the United States, Sergeant Reckless lived at Camp Pendleton, near San Diego. She had four foals. Reckless died in 1968. She was buried with full military honors.

A statue of Reckless was unveiled in 2013 at the National Museum of the Marine Corps in Virginia. Similar statues honor the memory of Reckless at Camp Pendleton and at Kentucky Horse Park in Lexington, Kentucky. A monument to Reckless also stands in South Korea at the site of the Battle of Outpost Vegas.

In 1997, *LIFE* magazine named Reckless one of America's 100 greatest heroes.

Sgt Reckless

Glossary

ammunition
(am-yuh-NIH-shuhn)
bullets and other objects that
can be fired from weapons

amputate (AM-pyuh-tayt)
to cut off someone's arm,
leg, or other body part due to
damage or disease

army reserve
(AHR-mee ri-ZUHRV) people
with military training but
who are called to duty only
when needed

artillery (ar-TIL-uh-ree)
cannons and other large
guns designed to strike an
enemy from a distance

communist
(KAHM-yuh-nist)
a country or person following
a political system in which
there is no private property
and everything is owned and
controlled by the government

flak jacket (FLAK JAK-it)
a vest worn by soldiers
designed to protect them
from bullets or shrapnel

infantry (IN-fuhn-tree)
a group of soldiers trained to
travel and fight on foot

land mine (LAND MINE)
a small bomb hidden in
the ground that explodes if
someone steps or drives on it

prosthetic (pross-THET-ik)
an artificial body part, such
as an arm or leg

recoilless rifle
(ri-KOIL-is RAHY-fuhl)
a powerful gun used mainly
for shooting tanks or other
vehicles

shrapnel (SHRAP-nuhl)
sharp pieces of metal that
fly in all directions when
a bomb, explosive shell, or
land mine explodes

Read More

Hale, Nathan. *Cold War Correspondent: A Korean War Tale*. New York: Amulet Books, 2021.

McCormick, Patricia. *Sergeant Reckless: The True Story of the Little Horse Who Became a Hero*. New York: HarperCollins Publishers, 2017.

Yomtov, Nel. *Cher Ami Comes Through: Heroic Carrier Pigeon of World War I*. North Mankato, MN: Capstone, 2023.

Internet Sites

Britannica Kids: Korean War
kids.britannica.com/kids/article/Korean-War/353347

History: The Four-Legged Marine Who Became a Korean War Hero
history.com/news/the-four-legged-marine-who-became-a-korean-war-hero

Sgt Reckless
sgtreckless.com/

About the Author

Bruce Berglund was a history professor for 19 years. He taught courses on ancient and modern history, war and society, and the history of Korea, China, and Japan. He has traveled to many countries to research history books, including Korea for the 2018 Winter Olympics. He is not good at riding horses and has been thrown off twice.

About the Illustrator

Mark Simmons is a freelance illustrator and cartoonist based in San Francisco. His past work includes comics for publishers such as Capstone, Behrman House, and Rebellion, as well as animation and advertising storyboards, animated operas, and other strange things. He also teaches comic art, figure drawing, and wildlife illustration for local zoos, schools, and museums. He loves animals of all kinds, especially bugs! For more info, visit www.ultimatemark.com.